THE FIVE POINTS OF CHRISTIANITY

A Biblical Defense of Calvinism

With a Response to the Opposite
Doctrines of Arminianism

by
Greg Loren Durand

sola fide
PUBLISHERS
www.solafidepublishers.com

The Five Points of Christianity:
A Biblical Defense of Calvinism
by Greg Loren Durand

Second Edition
Copyright © 1997, 2017
by Greg Loren Durand
All rights reserved.

All quoted Scripture has been taken from the New King James Version, unless otherwise indicated.

Published by Sola Fide Publishers
P.O. Box 2027 Toccoa, Georgia 30577
www.solafidepublishers.com

Cover and Interior by Magnolia Graphic Design
www.magnoliagraphicdesign.com

ISBN-13: 978-0978602239
ISBN-10: 0978602234

Printed in the United States of America

. . . [T]he pious mind does not devise for itself any kind of God, but looks alone to the one true God; nor does it feign for him any character it pleases, but is contented to have him in the character in which he manifests himself.

— *John Calvin*

CONTENTS

INTRODUCTION

In 1989, Zondervan Publishing House released what was proclaimed by many to be one of the best defenses of "Arminianism" to be written in recent years. Edited by the late Clark H. Pinnock, *The Grace of God/The Will of Man* was a collection of essays written by leading Arminian scholars who argued in unison against the Reformed theology commonly known as "Calvinism," denouncing it as a rationalistic system which denies the clear teachings of the Bible.

Pinnock, who earned his Ph.D. from the University of Manchester, and was himself a defector from the Calvinist camp, opened the book with a detailed retelling of his "pilgrimage from Augustine to Arminius." Beginning with his rejection of the doctrine of the "Perseverance of the Saints," which he referred to as "likely the weakest link in Calvinian logic, scripturally speaking,"[1] Pinnock made an eloquent attempt to dispel the "dark shadow" of Calvinism, claiming that it blinds people to the clear salvific teaching of Scripture.

---

1. Clark H. Pinnock, "From Augustine to Arminius: A Pilgrimage in Theology," *The Grace of God/The Will of Man* (Grand Rapids, Michigan: Zondervan Publishing House, 1989), page 17.

Baptist minister Laurence M. Vance was equally harsh in his opposition to Calvinism:

> Nothing will deaden a church or put a young man out of the ministry any more than an adherence to Calvinism. Nothing will foster pride and selfishness as will an affection for Calvinism. Nothing will destroy holiness and spirituality as an attachment to Calvinism. There is no greater violator of every hermeneutical, contextual, analytical, and exegetical interpretation of Scripture than Calvinism.[2]

Most Arminians, of course, would not be so bombastic in their rejection of Reformed theology, and some have suggested that both Calvinism and Arminianism are really two sides of the same coin, being "very close to each other in substance."[3] It is said that while Calvinism places an emphasis upon God's sovereignty and justice, Arminianism focuses upon His infinite love for mankind. Debate between the two theological camps is therefore often repudiated as "anachronistic" and "insensitive,"[4] and an appeal for "balance" is often heard from those who seek to blur the line of distinction between them.[5] However, as we shall see, such

---

2. Laurence M. Vance, *The Other Side of Calvinism* (Pensacola, Florida: Vance Publications, 1991), page viii.

3. William J. Abraham, "Predestination and Assurance," *The Grace of God/The Will of Man*, page 231.

4. Abraham, *ibid*.

5. There are indeed those who have embraced Arminianism who clearly see the contrast between it and Calvinism. For example, scholar Terry L. Miethe, a staunch opponent of Reformation theology, stated, ". . . [T]he differences are quite major! They are really the most severe differences possible . . . philosophically, perhaps ultimately also psycho-

a plea is made in gross ignorance, not only of what Arminianism necessarily implies when its doctrines are drawn out to their logical conclusion, but of what the Bible says about the vital subject of God's redemptive work in behalf of fallen men.

According to Silas Henn, "By many, the Calvinistic controversy has been considered as long since settled, and comparatively few in these times, amid such enlightened views of Christianity, dare to proclaim, openly and without disguise, the peculiar tenets of John Calvin."[6] It is a common misconception that Calvinism originated in the mind of a sixteenth-century French rationalist who thought more highly of burning his theological dissenters at the stake than of engaging in a simple, Spirit-led study of the Bible.[7] This distorted caricature of John Calvin is quite popular in Arminian circles, despite the fact that his own writings abundantly attest to his respect for, and subjection to, the inspired Scriptures:

> If true religion is to beam upon us, our principle must be, that it is necessary to begin with heavenly teaching, and that it is impossible for any man to obtain even the minutest portion of right and sound doctrine without being a disciple

---

logically, about the nature of God, the nature of man, the teaching of Scripture, and (many times) man's responsibility to his fellow man" ("The Universal Power of the Atonement," *Grace of God/Will of Man*, page 91).

6. Silas Henn, quoted by Iain Murray, *The Forgotten Spurgeon* (Edinburgh, Scotland: The Banner of Truth Trust, 1978), pages 53-54).

7. Dan Corner, "Murderer And Heretic John Calvin Burned Michael Servetus At The Stake," www.evangelicaloutreach.org/michael-servetus.htm

of Scripture. Hence the first step in true knowledge is taken, when we reverently embrace the testimony which God has been pleased therein to give of Himself. For not only does faith, full and perfect faith, but all correct knowledge of God, originate in obedience.[8]

Calvin's purpose, and that of all the Reformers of the Sixteenth Century, was not to "form new and unheard-of revelations, or to coin a new form of doctrine,"[9] but to return the Christian Church to the pure Gospel upon which it was originally founded. Though his presentation of biblical truths was often accomplished in a very logical manner, intellectualism for the mere sake of it was never his intention. His was a theology that was meant to turn men from an improper view of themselves, and to cultivate within the hearts of his readers a deep reverence and worship for the gracious God whom he preached. According to Calvin, ". . . [T]he knowledge of God which we are invited to cultivate is not that which, resting satisfied with empty speculation, only flutters in the brain, but a knowledge which will prove substantial and fruitful wherever it is duly perceived, and rooted in the heart."[10]

The theological structure of Calvinism is commonly known by the acronym "T-U-L-I-P" – "*T*otal Depravity," "*U*nconditional Election," "*L*imited Atonement," "*I*rresistible Grace," and "*P*erseverance of the Saints." What is *not* com-

---

8. John Calvin, *Institutes of the Christian Religion* (Grand Rapids, Michigan: Wm. B. Eerdman's Publishing Company, 1989), Book I, Chapter VI:2.

9. Calvin, *ibid.*, Chapter IX:1.

10. Calvin, *ibid.*, Chapter V:9.

monly known is that the systematization of these five points was not Calvin's idea, but that of the Synod of Dordt in 1618. This council was convened several years after Calvin's death to respond to the assertions of the 1610 manifesto entitled the Remonstrance. The framers of this document, Simon Episcopious and John Uytenbogaert, two professed followers of Dutch theologian Jacob (James) Arminius, asserted that man is not so corrupted by sin that he cannot exercise faith on his own, that God "predestined" believers to salvation on the basis of His foresight of their faith, that Christ's death was in behalf of all men without exception, and that men not only can resist the "wooing" of the Spirit, but that they, in a post-regenerational state, can also sin to such an extent as to forfeit their salvation.[11]

The Synod of Dordt denounced the Remonstrance as a revival of the heretical teachings of the fifth-century British monk, Pelagius.[12] The so-called "five points of Calvinism,"

---

11. See Appendix Two: "Was Arminius an Arminian?"

12. Pelagius, who was the target of many of Augustine's polemical works, categorically denied that men were inherently wicked as a result of the fall of Adam. Instead, he believed that, in his disobedience, Adam merely served as a bad example to mankind. The sin nature, according to Pelagius, was neither transmitted to his descendants nor was his guilt imputed to them (Louis Berkhof, *History of Christian Doctrines* [Grand Rapids, Michigan: Wm. B. Eerdman's Publishing Company, 1937], pages 136-137; John Ferguson, *Pelagius: An Historical and Theological Study* [New York, AMS Press, n.d.], pages 96-97). The teachings of Pelagius thus bore the underlying implication that man is not so much in need of a Savior as merely a good example (Philip Schaff, *History of the Christian Church* [Grand Rapids, Michigan: Wm. B. Eerdman's Publishing Company, 1910], Volume III, page 815). Consequently, the heretical speculation arose that, in order to act in Adam's place as a true example of righteousness, Christ must have had the ability to sin, but He merely

which will be discussed in detail in the following pages, were therefore formulated in response to the Arminian insistence that fallen man plays a necessary role in his own salvation. Demanding strict adherence to Scripture, the Synod asserted, as did Calvin, that the salvation of sinners is solely an act of God's divine mercy and a bestowal of unmerited grace upon those who do not seek it, and, as such, is an irrevocable gift.[13]

What has raged within the professing Christian Church for so long must therefore be viewed, not merely as a non-essential debate between two differing, yet equally legitimate, systems of Bible interpretation, but as a contest between truth

---

chose not to do so.

Pelagianism was condemned as heresy in 416 at the Council of Milevis, again in 418 at the Council of Carthage, and also in 431 at the Council of Ephesus. In its place, "Semi-Pelagianism" sprang up, which in turn was condemned in 529 at the Council of Orange. This position attempted to place itself between the two "extremes" of Pelagianism and Augustinianism by declaring that, although man is indeed adversely effected by the Fall, he is morally diseased or crippled, but not totally depraved. The Semi-Pelagians rejected the concept of absolute predestination, asserting instead that God's saving grace is only given to a man after he has taken the initial step by exercising his free will in believing the Gospel. This, of course, is precisely what Arminianism teaches, thus establishing the indisputable theological link between much of modern-day Evangelicalism and the fourth-century heretic, Pelagius. As Loraine Boettner pointed out, "The ancestry of Arminianism can be traced back to Pelagianism as definitely as can that of Calvinism be traced back to Augustinianism. Arminianism in its radical and more fully developed forms is essentially a recrudescence of Pelagianism" (*The Reformed Doctrine of Predestination* [Nutley, New Jersey: Presbyterian and Reformed Publishing Company, 1932], page 47).

13. See Appendix One: "The Canons of Dordt."

and heresy. It is, in fact, a battle between the true and glorious Gospel and an accursed counterfeit (Galatians 1:6-9). In the words of the late Charles Spurgeon:

> I have my own private opinion that there is no such thing as preaching Christ and Him crucified, unless we preach what is nowadays called Calvinism. It is a nickname to call it Calvinism; Calvinism is the gospel, and nothing else. I do not believe we can preach the gospel . . . unless we preach the sovereignty of God in His dispensation of grace; nor unless we exalt the electing, unchangeable, eternal, immutable, conquering love of Jehovah; nor do I think we can preach the gospel unless we base it upon the special and particular redemption of His elect and chosen people which Christ wrought out upon the Cross; nor can I comprehend a gospel which lets saints fall away after they are called. Such a gospel I abhor.[14]

---

14. Charles Haddon Spurgeon, *C. H. Spurgeon's Autobiography* (Edinburgh, Scotland: The Banner of Truth Trust, 1962), Volume I, page 168.

CHAPTER ONE
Total Depravity

Fallen Man's Awareness of Sin

> ... [I]n every age, he who is most forward in extolling the excellence of human nature, is received with the loudest applause. But be this heralding of human excellence what it may, by teaching men to rest in themselves, it does nothing more than fascinate by its sweetness, and, at the same time, so delude as to drown in perdition all who assent to it.[1]

John Calvin was absolutely correct. The discussion of sin has never been popular, and it is even less so in our own day. Many modern sermons are little more than self-help pep talks filled with references to the "good in every man" and exhortations to "think positively" about oneself, while the biblical picture of man as a hell-deserving sinner is downplayed and largely discarded as an outdated relic from the unenlightened past. For example, the late Dr. Robert Schuller, former pastor of the Crystal Cathedral in Garden Grove, California and host of the "Hour of Power" broad-

---

1. Calvin, *Institutes*, Book II, Chapter 1:2.

cast, said, "I don't think anything has been done in the name of Christ and under the banner of Christianity that has proven more destructive to human personality and, hence, counterproductive to the evangelism enterprise, than the often crude, uncouth, and unchristian strategy of attempting to make people aware of their lost and sinful condition."[2] By his own admission, Schuller's approach to evangelism is one "that begins and ends with a recognition of every person's hunger for glory."[3] This "hunger," which the Bible simply describes as satanic pride (Isaiah 14:12-15), is the driving force behind the virtual deluge of heretical teachings in modern Evangelicalism today, including "possibility thinking," "positive confession," "health and wealth," etc. The sinful heart of man, even when it has been regenerated by the Holy Spirit, does not easily submit to the notion that it is "undone" and "wretched" (Isaiah 6:5; Romans 7:24) and that it has no hope or life apart from Christ.

This stubborn refusal of man to face the truth about himself is also the rotten seed that lies at the very root of Arminianism. Just as "every bad tree bears bad fruit" (Matthew 7:17), churches in which Arminian theology has

---

2. Robert H. Schuller, *Christianity Today*, August 10, 1984, pages 23-24. Schuller died in 2015, only three years after his 57-year-old ministry was shattered by bankruptcy, lawsuits, and family in-fighting. His mantle thereafter fell upon Joel Osteen, the son of a Southern Baptist pastor who rose from obscurity to build a "positive thinking" empire in Houston, Texas with a membership of 43,000. Like Schuller before him, Osteen also refuses to discuss sin or judgment, focusing instead on helping his audience to achieve self-fulfillment and their "best life now."

3. Robert H. Schuller, *Self Esteem: The New Reformation* (Waco, Texas: Word Books, 1982), page 27.

prevailed have produced thousands of spiritually lifeless professors of religion, who are more concerned with physical health, self-esteem, and temporal happiness than they are with obeying the commandments of God. Licentiousness abounds in such congregations for "if sin becomes a trifle, virtue will be a toy."[4]

W. J. Seaton rightly noted, "If we have deficient and light views about sin, then we are liable to have defective views regarding the means necessary for the salvation of the sinner."[5] By teaching sinners that their salvation depends upon their own choice, Arminian evangelism has spawned entire generations of professing believers who, though resting in their "simple faith," may very well not be saved at all. This problem, however, is not nearly so prevalent where Calvinism is faithfully preached and accepted.

Is Man Totally Depraved Or Just Deprived?

> When I consider Your heavens, the work of Your fingers, the moon and the stars, which You have ordained, what is man that You are mindful of him, and the son of man that You visit him? (Psalm 8:3-4)

The Scriptures teach that man was created by God in His image and likeness (Genesis 1:27). This similitude is seen in man's ability to reason (Isaiah 1:18) and to exercise personal volition (Joshua 24:15). Thus, the one thing that man has in common with his Creator is personhood. In his original state,

---

4. Spurgeon, quoted by Murray, *Forgotten Spurgeon*, page 38.

5. W. J. Seaton, *The Five Points of Calvinism* (Edinburgh, Scotland: The Banner of Truth Trust, 1970), page 9.

the first man, Adam, enjoyed what is referred to as "unconfirmed creaturely holiness." As such, his will was completely free to choose to obey or to disobey God's command. However, the biblical view of man does not end there:

> In this upright state, man possessed freedom of will, by which, if he chose, he was able to obtain eternal life. . . . Adam, therefore, might have stood if he chose, since it was only by his own will that he fell; but it was because his will was pliable in either direction, and he had not received constancy to persevere, that he so easily fell. Still he had a free choice of good and evil; and not only so, but in the mind and will there was the highest rectitude, and all the organic parts were duly framed to obedience, until man corrupted its good properties, and destroyed himself.[6]

In addition to the ruin of his own soul, the disobedience of Adam, acting as the progenitor and representative head of mankind, resulted in the corruption of his posterity as well. Thus, the doctrine of "original sin" declares that, since all men were "seminally present" in Adam their "federal head," all have not only inherited the pollution of sin through physical generation, but have been imputed with his guilt through the righteous judgment of God:

> . . . [T]hrough one man sin entered the world, and death through sin, and thus death spread to all men, because all sinned – (For until the law sin was in the world, but sin is not imputed when there is no law. Nevertheless death reigned from Adam to Moses, even over those who had not sinned according to the likeness of the transgression

---

6. Calvin, *Institutes*, Book I, Chapter 15:8.

of Adam, who is a type of Him who was to come). . . .

Therefore, as through one man's offense judgment came to all men, resulting in condemnation, even so through one Man's righteous act the free gift came to all men, resulting in justification of life. For as by one man's disobedience many were made sinners, so also by one Man's obedience many will be made righteous (Romans 5:12-14, 18-19).

Few churches or denominations claiming to be orthodox would deny that man's nature is affected to some degree by original sin.[7] The differences exist, however, in the definition of this fallenness as well as its extent in each man. Is man utterly corrupt, or does he merely have an inclination towards evil? As always, we must let the Scriptures speak for themselves:

Then the LORD saw that the wickedness of man was great in the earth, and that every intent of the thoughts of his heart was only evil continually (Genesis 6:5).

The heart is deceitful above all things, and desperately wicked; who can know it? (Jeremiah 17:9)

As it is written: "There is none righteous, no, not one;

---

7. Dr. Robert Schuller, however, was one example of the extreme to which the ancient Pelagian denial of original sin has infected the modern pulpit. In his book, *Self-Esteem: The New Reformation*, he referred to the core of "original sin" as a "lack of trust," claiming that human beings "are fearful, not bad" (pages 63-67). It is important to note that Schuller was an ordained minister of the Reformed Church in America and even wrote his doctoral thesis on Calvin's *Institutes*. Unlike most Arminians, he fully comprehended the Reformed theology he was rejecting, and thus, in his case, the label of heretic is warranted.

there is none who understands; there is none who seeks after God. They have all turned aside; they have together become unprofitable; there is none who does good, no, not one."

"Their throat is an open tomb; with their tongues they have practiced deceit";

"The poison of asps is under their lips";

"Whose mouth is full of cursing and bitterness."

"Their feet are swift to shed blood; destruction and misery are in their ways; and the way of peace they have not known."

"There is no fear of God before their eyes" (Romans 3:10-18).

This I say, therefore, and testify in the Lord, that you should no longer walk as the rest of the Gentiles walk, in the futility of their mind, having their understanding darkened, being alienated from the life of God, because of the ignorance that is in them, because of the blindness of their heart; who, being past feeling, have given themselves over to lewdness, to work all uncleanness with greediness (Ephesians 4:17-19).

Man in his fallen state is not only spiritually dead by nature (Colossians 2:13), but is also judicially dead and under a curse (Colossians 3:10). Furthermore, men are "alienated and enemies in [their] mind[s] by wicked works" (Colossians 1:21). The terrible effects of sin are seen primarily in the mind, which is the seat of the will and the emotions, and it is there that the root of man's rebellion against God is discovered:

For the wrath of God is revealed from heaven against all ungodliness and unrighteousness of men, who suppress the truth in unrighteousness, because what may be known of God is manifest in them, for God has shown it to them. . . .

[B]ecause, although they knew God, they did not glorify Him as God, nor were thankful, but became futile in their thoughts, and their foolish hearts were darkened. . . .

And even as they did not like to retain God in their knowledge, God gave them over to a debased mind, to do those things which are not fitting. . . . (Romans 1:18-19, 21, 28)

According to this passage, men willfully suppress the knowledge of God by denying in their minds what the creation itself testifies of the Creator. Jesus Himself said that unregenerate men are "children of [their] father the devil" (John 8:44), and they will think and act accordingly. This brings us to what the Reformers called *total depravity*. According to John Calvin, ". . . [T]he whole man, from the crown of the head to the sole of his feet, is so deluged, as it were, that no part remains exempt from sin, and, therefore, everything which proceeds from him is imputed as sin."[8] This, however, is not to say that each man is as evil as he could be or that he will always act in each and every circumstance in the worst way possible, but that the stain of sin has extended to every aspect of his nature. Sin is not merely what man *does*; sin is what he *is*. Hence, though fallen man is still capable of temporal good, it is impossible for him to earn the favor of an infinitely holy God by anything he may do: "But we are all like an unclean thing, and all our righteousnesses are like filthy rags; we all fade as a leaf, and

---

8. Calvin, *Institutes*, Book II, Chapter 2:9.

our iniquities, like the wind, have taken us away" (Isaiah 64:6).

The Myth of Free Will

One of the main points of contention between Arminians and Calvinists is that of the free will of man. Is the will of man truly autonomous, or is it subject to exterior influences? Does man choose God, or does God choose man? Is salvation ultimately determined by man, or is God at all times in sovereign control?

Arminian author Richard Rice wrote, "Instead of attributing everything that happens to the sovereign will of God, Arminians insist that human beings have a capacity for genuine choice and self-determination. In particular, they are free to accept or reject God's offer of salvation."[9] Arminians such as Rice categorically deny that man, in and of himself, is incapable of choosing eternal life in Christ Jesus. Arminian evangelism is therefore riddled with phrases such as "make a decision for Christ," "invite Jesus into your heart," "make Jesus the Lord of your life," etc.[10] For example, well-

---

9. Richard Rice, "Divine Foreknowledge and Free Will Theism," *Grace of God/Will of Man*, page 123.

10. Such slogans are certainly nothing new, and were also prevalent in the days of Charles Spurgeon. Greatly troubled by the unbiblical system of altar calls and "enquiry rooms," Spurgeon wrote:

> The gospel is, "Believe on the Lord Jesus Christ, and thou shalt be saved." If we think we shall do more good by substituting another exhortation for the gospel command, we shall find ourselves landed in serious difficulties. If, for a moment, our improvements seem to produce a larger result than the old gospel, it will be the growth of mushrooms, it may even be the growth of toadstools; but it is not the growth of trees

known evangelist Billy Graham wrote, "Placing your faith in Christ means that first you must make a choice. . . . In order not to be condemned you must make a choice – you must choose to believe."[11]

Before we examine the theological problems with Graham's statement, we must first clear up some of the misconceptions regarding the will of man. As mentioned before, one important characteristic of man is the ability to exercise his will. However, this is not to say that the will *is* the man, nor does it mean that the man is, in any way, subject to his will. Since the mind or heart of man is the seat of the will, it is therefore the man's nature which determines what he will choose. Jonathan Edwards explained: "In every act . . . of the will, there is some preponderation of the mind or inclination, one way rather than another. . . . It is the strongest motive which determines the will."[12]

Natural abilities also play an important role in what a man chooses. For example, a man standing atop a twenty-story building may wish he could fly. However, if he is in possession of a sound mind, he knows that he is, by nature, incapable of this feat and that he will plunge to his death if he throws himself over the edge. Thus, the desire to preserve his own life overrules his wish to fly, and his choice is made accordingly. Our Lord stated, "For from within, out of the heart of men, proceed evil thoughts, adulteries, forni-

---

of the Lord (quoted by Murray, *Forgotten Spurgeon*, page 95).

11. Billy Graham, *How To Be Born Again* (Waco, Texas: Word Books, 1977), page 193.

12. Jonathan Edwards, *Freedom of the Will* (New Haven, Connecticut: Yale University Press, 1957), Volume I, pages 1-2.

cations, murders, thefts, covetousness, wickedness, deceit, lewdness, an evil eye, blasphemy, pride, foolishness. All these evil things come from within and defile a man" (Mark 7:21-23). Elsewhere, Scripture tells us that Jesus would not accept the testimonies of many of those who claimed to believe in Him because "He knew what was in man" (John 2:25). The heart of man is oriented toward sin, and so, everything which proceeds from it, including the choices it makes, cannot be anything but sin. Fallen man cannot choose spiritual good any more than he can choose to fly like a bird.

It may be helpful to use the illustration of a terminal patient confined to a hospital bed. On the nightstand beside him is a bottle of pills which, if taken, will save his life. However, our illustration must not end there. Let us also say that the man is blind, so he cannot see the bottle; he is paralyzed, so he cannot reach for the bottle; and, above all, he hates the doctor who prescribed the medicine. What then will the man do? He will simply lie there until he dies because his desires and his incapacitated condition prevent him from choosing to do anything else.

When presented with the Gospel, the hearer has only two options from which to choose. The first is to reject Christ and continue in a life of rebellion against God. The second is to fall at the foot of the cross in repentance for leading just such a life. Not at all unlike the man in the hospital bed, the hearer of the evangelical message will make a choice between the two options based upon his predispositions and abilities. Since the Bible declares that the ruling disposition of the unregenerate mind is "only evil continually," it is really quite futile to instruct such people to "choose to believe." Indeed, no man can choose to believe in the One whom his own nature causes him to despise and rebel against, and he is powerless to do anything towards the betterment of his spiritual condition. In the words of Charles Hodge:

> No more soul-destroying doctrine could well be devised than the doctrine that sinners can regenerate themselves, and repent and believe just when they please. . . . As it is a truth both of Scripture and of experience that the unrenewed man can do nothing of himself to secure his salvation, it is essential that he should be brought to a practical conviction of that truth. When thus convinced, and not before, he seeks help from the only source whence it can be obtained.[13]

Simply put, fallen man does not seek God's grace because he *has no desire* to seek God's grace, and is content to remain in sin. Being spiritually dead, he cannot see (John 3:3), hear (John 8:43-44), or understand (1 Corinthians 2:14) the things of God. As pointed out by Loraine Boettner, "Fallen man is so morally blind that he uniformly prefers and chooses evil instead of good."[14] In the very essence of his being, man is, until freed by divine intervention, a slave to sin (Romans 6:16), his desires and thoughts being completely controlled by his sinful nature (Ephesians 2:3). This fact is brought out in the following words of Paul:

---

13. Charles Hodge, *Systematic Theology* (Grand Rapids, Michigan: Wm. B. Eerdman's Publishing Company, 1993), Volume II, page 277.

14. Loraine Boettner, *The Reformed Doctrine of Predestination* (Nutley, New Jersey: Presbyterian and Reformed Publishing Company, 1932), page 63.

For those who live according to the flesh set their minds on the things of the flesh, but those who live according to the Spirit, the things of the Spirit. For to be carnally minded is death, but to be spiritually minded is life and peace. Because the carnal mind is enmity against God; for it is not subject to the law of God, nor indeed can be. So then, those who are in the flesh cannot please God (Romans 8:5-8).

It is important therefore to preface any discussion of God's sovereignty and human freedom with the question which lies at the very heart of the Calvinist-Arminian debate: Is fallen man really and completely spiritually dead? If he is, as the Bible clearly teaches, then any argument attempted in favor of Arminianism, whether it be derived from reason or an isolated biblical text, is necessarily wrong.

The Will of Man is Both Free and Bound

Charles Spurgeon once said, "I have heard some men talk as if the strength of free-will, of human nature, was sufficient to carry men to heaven. Free-will has carried many souls to hell, but never a soul to heaven yet. . . . O Sirs, I dread above all things that throughout eternity, you will be left to your own free wills."[15] Based on Scripture, it is the conviction of the Calvinist that fallen man's will is indeed free, but at the same time, it is bound. Man remains a free moral agent in that he is still able to make choices, but what he will choose is ultimately determined by his own nature.

---

15. Charles Haddon Spurgeon, *Metropolitan Tabernacle Pulpit* (London: Passmore & Alabaster, 1888), Volume XXXIV.

Reformed soteriology categorically denies that man may, by the exercise of his own free will, repent of his sins and believe in Christ, and thus be saved. If the biblical description of total depravity is to be maintained, then it must follow that the inherent wickedness of man prevents him from either seeking God, or from submitting himself to His laws. Apart from regeneration, man's will is perpetually bound to choose sin which, though detrimental to his eternal soul, is nevertheless pleasing to him. Thus, man does not continue in sin to ultimate damnation by coercion from without, but by the inward exercise of his own agency, which, though free, is nevertheless determined by his fallen spiritual condition:

> Man, since he was corrupted by the fall, sins not forced or unwilling, but voluntarily, by a most forward bias of the mind; not by violent compulsion, or external force, but by the movement of his passion; and yet such is the depravity of his nature, that he cannot move and act except in the direction of evil.[16]

> I hold in my hand a book. I release it; what happens? It falls. In which direction? Downwards; always downwards. Why? Because, answering the law of gravity, its own weight sinks it. Suppose I desire that book to occupy a position three feet higher; then what? I must lift it; a power outside of that book must raise it. Such is the relationship which fallen man sustains toward God. Whilst Divine power upholds him, he is preserved from plunging still deeper into sin; let that power be withdrawn, and he falls – his own weight (of sin) drags him down. God does not push him down, anymore than I did that book. Let all

---

16. Calvin, *Institutes*, Book II, Chapter 3:5.

Divine restraint be removed, and every man is capable of becoming, would become, a Cain, a Pharoah, a Judas. How then is the sinner to move heavenwards? By an act of his own will? Not so. A power outside of himself must grasp hold of him and lift him every inch of the way. The sinner *is* free, but free in one direction only – free to fall, free to sin (emphasis in original).[17]

This concept should not seem so strange to the ear of the Christian, for God Himself is one whose will is both free and bound. Because His nature is holy, He can do nothing but that which is holy. Consequently, He cannot do that which is evil – not merely because He chooses not to, but because His own nature renders such action impossible (Hebrews 6:18).[18] And yet, His righteous acts remain worthy of praise because He, of His own good will, has *chosen* to perform them. Thus, God is bound to freely act in accordance with His own holiness.

Likewise, the devil can do nothing but evil, but this he does by his own choice and is thus deserving of God's

---

17. Arthur W. Pink, *The Sovereignty of God* (Grand Rapids, Michigan: Baker Book House, 1984), pages 135-136.

18. Some Arminians will argue, however, that to say that God cannot do something is to put unbiblical restrictions on His omnipotence. Consequently, according to Stephen T. Davis, ". . . [I]t is possible for God to do evil," and "God has the ability to tell a lie" (*Logic and the Nature of God* [Grand Rapids, Michigan: Wm. B. Eerdman's Publishing Company, 1983], pages 2, 96). Davis also wrote of his abandonment of "the notion of God's timelessness . . . and the notion of God's immutability" (*ibid.,* page 2). It is incomprehensible how Davis and others who hold this view still view God as worthy of their worship, for such a corrupt theology cannot guarantee that, though holy today, God may change His mind and become a devil tomorrow.

judgment. To these examples, the Arminian is compelled by Scripture to assent. Why then is the inability of man to choose spiritual good so difficult to accept, especially when Scripture is so clear in this regard?

> "It is the Spirit who gives life; the flesh profits nothing. The words that I speak to you are spirit, and they are life. But there are some of you who do not believe. . . . Therefore I have said to you that no one can come to Me unless it has been granted to him by My Father" (John 6:63-65).

> "I am the vine, you are the branches. He who abides in Me, and I in him, bears much fruit; for without Me you can do nothing" (John 15:5).

The believer, on the other hand, is referred to as a "new creation" (2 Corinthians 5:17) because, as the object of God's special grace, he has been "renewed in the spirit of [his] mind" (Ephesians 4:23). Again, the mind of man is the primary focus here. In fact, the Greek word for repentance – μετάνοια (*metánoia*) – literally means "a change of mind."[19] Consequently, the heart of the converted sinner is "circumcised," and the "foreskin" of the mind's hostility toward God is "cut away" through repentance:

> Then the LORD your God will bring you to the land which your fathers possessed, and you shall possess it. He will prosper you and multiply you more than your fathers. And the LORD your God will circumcise your heart and the heart of your descendants, to love the LORD your God

---

19. W. E. Vine, *Expository Dictionary of New Testament Words* (McLean, Virginia: MacDonald Publishing Company, n.d.), pages 961-962.

with all your heart and with all your soul, that you may live (Deuteronomy 30:5-6).

For he is not a Jew who is one outwardly, nor is circumcision that which is outward in the flesh; but he is a Jew who is one inwardly; and circumcision is that of the heart, in the Spirit, not in the letter; whose praise is not from men but from God (Romans 2:28-29).

And you, being dead in your trespasses and the uncircumcision of your flesh, He has made alive together with Him, having forgiven you all trespasses (Colossians 2:13).

In short, the believer has been given a new heart that no longer continues to take pleasure in sin, but one that delights in pleasing God and glorifying Him alone (Romans 7:22). This inward change is known in theological terms as *regeneration*, which is that act of God by which "the principle of the new life is implanted in man, and the governing disposition of the soul is made holy."[20] According to the Bible, regeneration is a "good work" which is both begun and carried through to completion by God (Philippians 1:6). Men "become children of God," therefore, "not of blood, nor of the will of the flesh, nor of the will of man, but of God" (John 1:12-13). To insist, as Arminians do, that man's choice precedes regeneration is to rob God of the glory which is His alone in the salvation of sinners, for only He "can bring a clean thing out of an unclean" (Job 14:4).

---

20. Louis Berkhof, *Systematic Theology* (Grand Rapids, Michigan: Wm. B. Eerdman's Publishing Company, 1941), page 468.

The Bible Teaches That Saving Faith is a Gift

> . . . [M]an's contribution need not be in the form of
> actual deeds to his credit. It could be merely that he decides
> to respond favorably to the moving of the Holy Spirit in
> his heart. This makes salvation a joint effort.[21]

So wrote Laurence Vance in his attempted refutation
of Calvinism. Such a view is clearly synergistic. In other
words, God has devised the plan of redemption, but it is
ultimately man's own effort (his exercise of faith) that sets
the process of salvation into motion. However, since we
know from Hebrews 11:6 that "without faith it is impossible
to please [God]," how can it be that an unregenerate man
may exercise saving faith when the Apostle so clearly said
that such a man "cannot please God"? Obviously, this is an
absurd claim, especially since faith itself is described in
Scripture as a gift: "For by grace you have been saved
through faith, and that not of yourselves; it is the gift of God"
(Ephesians 2:8).

Arminians, of course, would object to this interpretation
of faith as a gift primarily on the grounds that the Greek
pronoun in Ephesians 2:8 is neuter in gender, while πίστις
(*pístis* – *faith*) is feminine. Therefore, according to Terry
Miethe, "it" must be in reference to salvation, not faith.[22]
However, what is overlooked in this argument is that
σωτηρία (*sōtería* – *salvation*) is also feminine, as is χάρις
(*cháris* – *grace*). The neuter pronoun τοῦτο (*touto* – *this* or *it*)
must therefore refer to θεοῦ τὸ δῶρον (*theou to dōron* – *the*

---

21. Vance, *Other Side of Calvinism*, page 300.

22. Miethe, "Universal Power," page 77.

gift of God). This passage describes faith as the instrument of saving grace, and since it is clearly stated that this is οὐκ ἐξ ὑμῶν (*ouk ek humōn* – literally *not out of yourselves*), faith must be included in God's gift.

Arminians also argue that since Christ commanded men in Mark 11:22 to "have faith in God," then either faith must be something that man is capable of producing within himself, or, as William Craig complained, God "would be demanding the impossible and then condemning them for failing to do it."[23] It may be helpful here to point out Jesus' command in John 20:22 to "receive the Holy Spirit." Surely this also would have been impossible for the disciples to do had the Holy Spirit not first been given to them. The Apostle Paul's rhetorical question, "[W]hat do you have that you did not receive?" (1 Corinthians 4:7), also serves to effectively silence this argument. Romans 12:3 likewise speaks of "the measure of faith" which God has dealt to believers, and Hebrews 12:2 speaks of Christ as "the author . . . of our faith." Thus, we must conclude that "not all have faith" (1 Thessalonians 3:2) because all men have not been *granted* faith by God.

In Galatians 5:22, faith is listed as one of the fruits of the indwelling Holy Spirit, and yet elsewhere we have our Lord's testimony that "a good tree cannot bear bad fruit, nor can a bad tree bear good fruit" (Matthew 7:18). Moreover, according to Romans 14:23, "whatever is not from faith is sin." Not only is the unregenerate sinner, in whom the Holy Spirit does not dwell, incapable of producing faith from

---

23. William L. Craig, "Middle Knowledge: A Calvinist/Arminian Rapproachment?", *Grace of God/Will of Man*, page 160.

within himself, but anything he does produce is accounted by God as sin. The complete bondage of fallen man to sin and his inability to believe the Gospel is therefore not an invention of Calvinism, but is an essential doctrine of Christianity. The Arminian concept of free will is indeed a "worldly maxim,"[24] for to declare that, apart from God's intervening grace, man is capable of choosing righteousness over unrighteousness is to deny what the Bible so plainly teaches, and to thus fall outside the pale of orthodoxy:

> ... [T]hose who, while they profess to be the disciples of Christ, still seek for free-will in man, notwithstanding of his being lost and drowned in spiritual destruction, labour under manifold delusion, making a heterogeneous mixture of inspired doctrine and philosophical opinions, and so erring as to both. . . .
>
> Those who invest us with more than we possess only add sacrilege to our ruin.[25]

Is the Doctrine of "Prevenient Grace" Biblical?

Prevenient grace – or *moral suasion*, as it is sometimes called – was popularized by John Wesley, who attempted to retain a belief in the total depravity of mankind and yet somehow avoid the doctrines of election and particular grace.[26] This doctrine is widely held today by Arminians

---

24. Spurgeon, quoted by Murray, *Forgotten Spurgeon*, page 61.

25. Calvin, *Institutes*, Book I, Chapter 15:8. See also Calvin, *ibid.*, Book II, Chapter 2:1.

26. Millard J. Erickson, *Christian Theology* (Grand Rapids, Michigan: Baker Book House, 1985), page 914.

seeking to do the same. For example, Henry Theissen wrote, "Since mankind is hopelessly dead in trespasses and sins and can do nothing to obtain salvation, God graciously restores to all men sufficient ability to make a choice in the matter of submission to Him. This is the salvation-bringing grace of God that has appeared to all men."[27] A. W. Tozer likewise wrote:

> Christian theology teaches the doctrine of prevenient grace, which, briefly stated, means that before a man can seek God, God must first have sought the man.
>
> Before a sinful man can think a right thought of God, there must have been a work of enlightenment done within him. Imperfect it may be, but a true work nonetheless, and the secret cause of all desiring and seeking and praying which may follow.[28]

It is difficult to understand how prevenient grace can be both "imperfect" *and* "a true work" of God, for surely nothing that a perfect Being accomplishes can fall short of His own perfection. If God's grace is imperfect, what assurance can the believer possibly have that the security of the salvation which it has wrought is not likewise imperfect? Fortunately, there is the rare Arminian writer who will admit that no such doctrine of "prevenient grace" may be found anywhere in the Bible. Clark Pinnock wrote, " . . . [T]he Bible has no developed doctrine of universal prevenient grace,

---

27. Henry C. Theissan, *Introductory Lectures in Systematic Theology* (Grand Rapids, Michigan: Wm. B. Eerdman's Publishing Company, 1959), pages 344-345.

28. A. W. Tozer, *The Pursuit of God* (Camp Hill, Pennsylvania: Christian Publications, Inc., 1982), page 11.

however convenient it would be for us if it did."[29]

The primary passage of Scripture used to support prevenient grace is John 1:9, which testifies of "the true Light which gives light to every man coming into the world." Thus, the illumination of God's saving grace is supposedly dispensed indiscriminately to all men without exception. This, however, cannot be a plausible interpretation of this verse when it is read in its proper context. In verse 5, we read, "And the light shines in the darkness, and the darkness did not comprehend it." The "darkness" here is obviously used metaphorically in reference to unbelievers, just as it is in 2 Corinthians 6:14-15. This idea is carried out further in the following verses: "And this is the condemnation, that the light has come into the world, and men loved darkness rather than light, because their deeds were evil. For everyone practicing evil hates the light and does not come to the light, lest his deeds should be exposed" (John 3:19-20).

In the final analysis, therefore, prevenient grace does not solve the problem which its proponents claim it does. One may shine a light upon a corpse all he wishes, but to no avail. Dead eyes simply cannot see. A loving whisper in the ear of a dead man will likewise never be heard. Therefore, to claim God touches the heart of the spiritually dead just enough to enable them to respond to His offer of eternal life is to either deny that they were really and truly dead to begin with, or that the life that God imparts is insufficient to generate any true spiritual vitality. Of course, neither of these options is consistent with the Scriptures:

---

29. Pinnock, "From Augustine to Arminius," page 22.

And you He made alive, who were dead in trespasses and sins, in which you once walked according to the course of this world, according to the prince of the power of the air, the spirit who now works in the sons of disobedience, among whom also we all once conducted ourselves in the lusts of our flesh, fulfilling the desires of the flesh and of the mind, and were by nature children of wrath, just as the others.

But God, who is rich in mercy, because of His great love with which He loved us, even when we were dead in trespasses, made us alive together with Christ (by grace you have been saved), and raised us up together, and made us sit together in the heavenly places in Christ Jesus, that in the ages to come He might show the exceeding riches of His grace in His kindness toward us in Christ Jesus (Ephesians 2:1-7).

CHAPTER TWO
Unconditional Election

Double Predestination: The "Horrible Decree"

The first and best discovery I made was that there was no "horrible decree" at all. Calvin had used this expression in connection with his belief that God in his sovereign good pleasure had predestined some people to be eternally lost for no fault of theirs. Calvin was compelled to say that because, if one thinks that God determines all that happens in the world . . . and not all are to be saved in the end . . . there is no way around it. . . . God wills whatever happens, so if there are to be lost people, God must have willed it. It was as logically necessary as it was morally intolerable.[1]

The subject under attack in the above paragraph is the doctrine of *reprobation*. This is the negative companion of *unconditional election*, the second point of Calvinism which we will discuss in this chapter. Both of these doctrines are to be found within the overall concept of *absolute predestination*, which is "that eternal act of God whereby He, in His

---

1. Pinnock, "From Augustine to Arminius," page 19.

37

sovereign good pleasure, and on account of no foreseen merit in them, chooses a certain number of men to be the recipients of special grace and eternal salvation."[2] Calvin himself described predestination as "the eternal decree of God, by which he determined with himself whatever he wished to happen with regard to every man. All are not created on equal terms, but some are preordained to eternal life, others to eternal damnation; and accordingly, as each has been created for one or other of these ends, we say that he has been predestined to life or to death."[3]

The doctrine of predestination, with its sub-doctrines of election and reprobation, cannot be properly understood apart from the biblical teachings regarding the condition of fallen man, for as Loraine Boettner rightly pointed out, it "follows by the most inescapable logic."[4] If totally depraved men cannot of themselves respond favorably to the Gospel, and yet some obviously do, in fact, believe and are saved, then no other conclusion remains than that their salvation is the result of God's sovereign choice. Obviously, then, the choosing, or election, of some to eternal life, necessitates the rejection, or reprobation, of others to eternal death. While the first implies positive action by God, as will be shown, the latter implies negative action. In other words, God directly acts upon some men so as to save them, and does not act upon others, thereby ensuring that they will be judged and damned for their own sinfulness.[5] Since He who acts or does

---

2. Berkhof, *Systematic Theology*, page 114.

3. Calvin, *Institutes*, Book III, Chapter XXI, Section 5.

4. Boettner, *Reformed Doctrine of Predestination*, page 95.

5. Perhaps John Gill was correct in suggesting that the term *rejection*

not act is eternal, so also is the foreordination of each man's destiny eternal, thus rendering both human belief *and* human unbelief necessary to God's decree. It is this fine, yet very important, distinction that is invariably misunderstood by the Arminian masses, who cannot relinquish the false assumption that Calvinists believe that God is the author of sin.[6]

In writing on predestination, John Calvin once stated, "The human mind, when it hears this doctrine, cannot restrain its petulance, but boils and rages as if aroused by the sound of a trumpet."[7] This is no less true in our own day simply because human nature has not changed over the last five hundred years. Fallen man's stubborn refusal to view himself as spiritually dead in sin is perhaps the sole reason for the existence of the Calvinist-Arminian debate. The late John Gerstner explained that the person who rejects predestination does so because "he invariably believes . . . [that] man apart from election is able to believe and be saved."[8] Ever since the fall of Adam and Eve, it has been an inherent flaw in man's nature to avoid honest self-evaluation. And yet, while "passing the buck" when it comes to his own sin, man is amazingly quick to take credit for what he perceives to be acts of personal righteousness. The companion doctrines of unconditional election and reprobation are so naturally

---

be substituted for *reprobation* due to the "wrong and frightful ideas" associated with the latter (*A Complete Body of Doctrinal and Practical Divinity* [Paris, Arkansas: The Baptist Standard Bearer, 1987], page 192).

6. See Appendix Three: "The Idolatry of Arminian Theology."

7. Calvin, *Institutes*, Book III, Chapter 23:1.

8. John Gerstner, *A Predestinarian Primer* (Grand Rapids, Michigan: Baker Book House, 1960), page 12.

abhorrent because they directly confront both of these fleshly impulses. Not only does the preaching of these doctrines force men to admit their guilt and helpless condition before God, but it also deprives them of the satisfaction of having a partnership in the work of salvation. Predestination leans obtrusively upon the weaknesses of the flesh and hangs ominously like a dark cloud over sinful man's imagined paradise. Thus, when brought face-to-face with God's absolute sovereignty, "the flesh whimpers . . . and begs like Agag for a little mercy."[9]

This unfortunate truth is perhaps no more clearly seen than in the writings of Clark Pinnock. Although he claimed to have been "converted" to Arminianism through a diligent study of the Scriptures, Pinnock repeatedly used such terms as "morally intolerable" and "morally loathsome" in his arguments against the doctrine of unconditional predestination,[10] and described his acceptance of the Arminian "alternative" as an "immense relief."[11] It would seem that, rather than actually being instructed by the Bible, Pinnock was instead driven to his conclusions by his own emotions. Sadly, such is the case with most adherents to Arminianism. Jerry Walls, for example, wrote the following:

> On the face of it, it does not seem right that God should choose to damn persons who were never free either to choose good or to obey God. It does not seem right that salvation and damnation are distributed solely on the basis of God's arbitrary will, independent of anything human

---

9. Tozer, *Pursuit of God*, page 101.

10. Pinnock, "From Augustine to Arminius," page 19.

11. Pinnock, *ibid.*, page 21.

beings do or do not do. . . .

[Calvinism] requires us to believe God is right in
unconditionally damning whomever he wills, even though
this deeply offends our sense of justice.[12]

Frank Schaeffer, son of the late Francis Schaeffer,
recently stated that the God of the Reformation "emerged
as a, if not *the*, Devil" (emphasis in original), and then went
on to write: "Ironically, the 'God' that the Calvinists invented
was also reduced to near impotence by theoretically being
portrayed as monstrously omnipotent. The Calvinist 'God'
was a great unfathomable Zeus-like computer in the sky who
arbitrarily saved some while damning others – an irrational,
perhaps berserk, Augustinian phenomenon no more loving
or predictable than a forest fire."[13]

Laurence Vance referred to predestination as "the most
obscene, vulgar, pagan, godless blasphemy that could ever
be uttered."[14] These men are merely following the example
of their predecessor, John Wesley, who likewise condemned
predestination for supposedly representing God "as worse
than the devil; more false, more cruel, and more unjust."[15]
This doctrine was even the subject of some of his satirical
poetry:

---

12. Jerry L. Walls, "Divine Commands, Predestination, and Moral
Intuition," *Grace of God/Will of Man*, pages 262-263, 265.

13. Frank Schaeffer, *Dancing Alone* (Brookline, Massachusetts: Holy
Cross Orthodox Press, 1994), pages 70, 87.

14. Vance, *Other Side of Calvinism*, page 159.

15. John Wesley, *The Works of John Wesley* (Grand Rapids, Michigan:
Baker Book House, 1979), Volume VII, page 382.

God, ever merciful and just,
    With newborn babes did Tophet fill;
Down into endless torments thrusts;
    Merely to show His sovereign will.
This is that "Horrible Decree"!
    This is that wisdom from beneath!
God (O detest the Blasphemy)
    Hath pleasure in the sinner's death.[16]

It is evident that this doctrine evokes a very strong emotional reaction in the mind of the Arminian, who, as J. I. Packer pointed out, "even in salvation cannot bear to renounce the delusion of being master of his fate and captain of his soul."[17] In discerning spiritual truth, the Christian, however, is never to be led by what "seems right" (Proverbs 14:12), or even "natural," but by the written Word of God alone. The accusation that "the Calvinist rams his doctrines of election and predestination into every conceivable Scripture text"[18] is certainly unfounded, for, as will be shown, the Bible clearly teaches these important doctrines.

The Logical Necessity of Absolute Predestination

In his essay, Clark Pinnock defined predestination as "God's setting goals for people rather than forcing them to

---

16. Wesley, quoted by Alan P. Sell, *The Great Debate* (Grand Rapids, Michigan: Baker Book House, 1982), page 72.

17. J. I. Packer, "Introductory Essay," in John Owen, *The Death of Death in the Death of Christ* (Edinburgh, Scotland: The Banner of Truth Trust, 1985), page 9.

18. Vance, *Other Side of Calvinism*, page 104.

enact the preprogrammed decrees,"[19] and "an all-inclusive set of goals and not an all-determining plan."[20] He then went on to interpret Romans 8:29 to mean that God's plan (or hope) for every man or woman is that they will be conformed to "the image of His Son," but that the decision "to go down that path" is ultimately theirs to make: "The banquet of salvation has been set for all people. God has provided plenteous redemption in the work of Christ, sufficient for the salvation of the entire race of sinners. All that remains for any individual to benefit from what was accomplished for him is to respond to the good news and enter into the new relationship with God that has been opened up for all persons."[21]

Pinnock's remarks would be heartily echoed by virtually every one of his fellow Arminians. For example, popular author and speaker Dave Hunt likewise voiced his objections to the Calvinist understanding of predestination by writing, "It would be a libel upon God's character (as well as a denial of the clear teaching of many Scriptures), to say that He is able, but unwilling, to save all."[22] Since this objection is a common one, let us examine the logic behind it. First of all, there are only three available options when dealing with God's plan of redemption. Either He is unwilling, yet quite *able*, to save all, or He is quite willing, yet *unable* to save all, or He is both willing *and* able. The first option (the Calvinist

---

19. Pinnock, "From Augustine to Arminius," page 20.

20. Pinnock, *ibid.*, page 21.

21. Pinnock, *ibid.*, page 19.

22. Dave Hunt, *What Ever Happened to Heaven?* (Eugene, Oregon: Harvest House, 1990), page 276.

position) is rejected by Hunt as a "libel upon God's character," and yet that is precisely the end result of the other two options. A God who is *willing* to save all, yet *unable* to do so for any reason whatsoever, as in the second option, cannot be the all-powerful God who has revealed Himself in the Scriptures. This is the position taken by the Arminian who insists that God's "desire" that all mankind be saved can be thwarted by the lack of faith on the part of the objects of His "affection." On the other hand, if the third option is true, and God is both willing *and* able to save all men, then, if the omnipotence of the Creator is not again to be called into question, all must surely be saved. Many Arminian writers have espoused this position while attempting to avoid the obvious heresy of Universalism which is the necessary consequence, and yet, in doing so, they must revert back to the second option when asked why all men are not ultimately saved after all. "Because they do not exercise faith in Christ," is the predictable answer – implying, of course, that God is not really *able* to save all men, but that He is only *willing* to do so.

Far from slandering the character of God, as the critics of Calvinism claim, the doctrine that God is quite able to save all, but is nevertheless selective in the bestowal of His grace, both upholds His omnipotence and His sovereignty. Surely God's love is not denigrated in any way by this proposal, but is magnified far beyond our comprehension. When we consider the terrible depths of the depravity of the human race, and the blasphemy and hatred that the Creator has patiently endured for six thousand years, it is amazing grace indeed that He should choose to save *anyone*. Like Pinnock, who complained that Calvinism teaches that men are con-

demned "for no fault of theirs," the Arminian often fails to
fully understand that God's infinite holiness is insulted every
day that wicked men continue to exist and by every breath
that proceeds from their nostrils. However, in His equally
infinite mercy, He has graciously selected some from among
this accursed mass to be recipients of His favor and to be
adopted into His own eternal family.

Hence, in the words of John Calvin, God "does not pay
a debt [to man], a debt which never can be due."[23] It is man
who is indebted to God, not vice versa, and it is therefore
no injustice on His part to extend pardon to some and to
withhold it from others. God's sovereign election of some
men for salvation is therefore wholly merciful, while His
reprobation of others to eternal damnation, though equally
sovereign, is wholly righteous. If the former group receive
what they did *not* deserve, and the latter what they *did*
deserve, how can this be denounced as injustice? It cannot
be. John Gill wrote:

> . . . [O]ur doctrine represents God as merciful, yea more
> merciful than that which is opposite to it; since, according
> to our doctrine, God, of His abundant grace and mercy,
> has determined to give pardoning, regenerating, and
> persevering grace to a certain number of men, whereby
> they shall be infallibly saved, when He denies it to others;
> whereas, according to the contrary scheme, God has not
> absolutely chosen one single person to salvation; but His
> choice proceeds upon their faith, repentance, and persever-
> ance; which also are left to the power and will of man; so
> that at most, the salvation of every man is precarious and

---

23. Calvin, *Institutes*, Book III, Chapter 21:1.

uncertain, nay, I will venture to say, entirely impossible.[24]

Arminians Misunderstand God's Foreknowledge

The primary biblical text which teaches the doctrine of predestination is Romans 8:29-30: "For whom He foreknew, He also predestined to be conformed to the image of His Son, that He might be the firstborn among many brethren. Moreover whom He predestined, these He also called; whom He called, these He also justified; and whom He justified, these He also glorified." Taken at face value, this passage alone should be sufficient to prove that God does indeed select some from the family of man upon whom to bestow His grace. The logical reverse of this is that He also rejects or passes over others, thus foreordaining them to eternal damnation. Such a conclusion, however, is unacceptable to the Arminian mind which cannot bear to think that a "God of love" would ever restrict salvation to but a few. Thus, a perversion of this passage is the only alternative left to "falling prey" to the "horrible decree" of Calvinism.

The typical Arminian response to the Apostle's words in the eighth chapter of Romans is to misinterpret the word *foreknow*. For example, W. E. Vine defined *foreknowledge* by stating that God "foreknows the exercise of faith which brings salvation."[25] Henry Thiessen likewise wrote, "By election we mean that sovereign act of God in grace whereby He chose in Christ Jesus for salvation all those whom He

---

24. John Gill, *The Cause of God and Truth* (Grand Rapids, Michigan: Sovereign Grace Publishers, 1971), page 151.

25. Vine, *Expository Dictionary*, page 459.

foreknew would accept Him."[26] In other words, God supposedly looked down through the corridors of time, foresaw
those who would freely exercise faith in His Son, and, on
that basis, elected them to salvation. The logical problems
with this interpretation are obvious. One might inquire of
the Arminian which came first – the sovereign election of
God or the autonomous choice of man? If the former, how
can the choice really be said to have been that of man's own
free will? If the latter, how can the election be said to have
been the sovereign prerogative of the Creator? There are
no adequate answers to these questions.[27]

However, if we apply the biblical definition of eternality

---

26. Theissen, *Introductory Lectures*, page 344.

27. R.P. Francisco Suarez offered the following as a possible answer:

> The efficacy of this call consists in this, that God, in His infinite
> wisdom foreseeing what each cause or will shall do in every event and
> occasion, if placed in it, also knows when and to which vocation each
> will shall give assent if it [the call] is given. Therefore, when He wills
> to convert a man He wills also to call him at that time and in that way
> in which He knows he will consent, and such a vocation is called
> efficacious because, although of itself it does not have an infallible effect,
> yet inasmuch as it is subject to such divine knowledge it shall infallibly
> have it (*De Concursu et Auxilio Dei* [Ludovicum Vives, 1856-1878; Carolo
> Berton, editor], III:14:9).

Thus, God's election of believers is not seen as effective in and of
itself, but only because He infallibly knows what circumstances will
effectively influence each man to respond favorably to His calling.
Though this explanation (known as *congruism*) attempts to deny the
Calvinist understanding of election in one way, it actually affirms it
in another. Whether the election itself is viewed as efficacious, or the
circumstances into which God places men so as to efficaciously influence
them towards conversion, the end result is that men are efficaciously
converted by God's sovereign will.

to God's election of believers, as we must in light of such passages as Ephesians 1:4 and Revelation 17:8, we are driven to conclude that such an election is utterly transcendent of time and therefore is not contingent in any way upon the actions or wills of finite men. Furthermore, the belief that God's omniscience merely refers to the ability to look forward in time is a complete misunderstanding of that particular attribute. The eternal God knows all things simply because He sees them as one collective present and therefore must have ordained them, either by His causative or His permissive will.[28]

---

28. Divine passivity should not be inferred from the term "permissive." There is no functional difference, but only a logical distinction, between God's causative and permissive will, for there is, in reality, but one eternal decree. As stated in the Westminster Confession:

> God from all eternity did by the most wise and holy counsel of his own will, freely and unchangeably ordain whatsoever comes to pass; yet so as thereby neither is God the author of sin; nor is violence offered to the will of the creatures, nor is the liberty or contingency of second causes taken away, but rather established (Chapter III:1).

> God the great Creator of all things does uphold, direct, dispose, and govern all creatures, actions, and things, from the greatest even to the least, by his most wise and holy providence, according to his infallible foreknowledge, and the free and immutable counsel of his own will, to the praise of the glory of his wisdom, power, justice, goodness, and mercy.
>
> Although, in relation to the foreknowledge and decree of God, the first Cause, all things come to pass immutably, and infallibly; yet, by the same providence, he orders them to fall out, according to the nature of second causes, either necessarily, freely, or contingently.
>
> God, in his ordinary providence, makes use of means, yet is free to work without, above, and against them, at his pleasure.
>
> The almighty power, unsearchable wisdom, and infinite goodness of God so far manifest themselves in his providence, that it extends itself even to the first fall, and all other sins of angels and men; and that not

Moreover, the Arminian interpretation falls apart when it is taken into consideration that the Greek verb προγι– νώσκω (*proginōskō – foreknow*) indicates much more than a simple precognition, as if God merely witnesses an event or an act (such as the exercise of faith) in advance. Even Charles Ryrie conceded to the Calvinists' interpretation of this word when he wrote, "God related Himself to people before time in some way so that there is a causative connection which makes foreknew practically equivalent to predestine or foreordain."[29] This meaning is clearly seen in the usage of the noun πρόγνωσις (*prognōsis – foreknowledge*) in Acts 2:23, where it is coupled with God's "determined purpose" regarding the crucifixion of Jesus Christ. This cannot be misconstrued to mean that the Father merely foreordained the death of His Son on the basis of His foreknowledge that it would happen, because the perpetrators of the great crime merely did "whatever [His] hand and [His] purpose determined before to be done" (Acts 4:28). The reference to Christ as " the Lamb slain from the foundation of the world" (Revelation 13:8) proves beyond all argument that God's foreknowledge, at least in this instance, is inseparable from His will, and must therefore be seen as causative and not derivative.

---

by a bare permission, but such as has joined with it a most wise and powerful bounding, and otherwise ordering, and governing of them, in a manifold dispensation, to his own holy ends; yet so, as the sinfulness thereof proceeds only from the creature, and not from God, who, being most holy and righteous, neither is nor can be the author or approver of sin (Chapter V:1-4).

29. Charles C. Ryrie, *Basic Theology* (Wheaton, Illinois: Victor Books, 1986), page 313.

It is apparent that the Greek verb προγινώσκω and its root verb γινώσκω are directly connected to the Hebrew word ידע (yada), which frequently suggests an intimate knowledge of, or a relationship with, a "familiar friend" or a "kins-man."[30] As such, this word was used to describe the marital relationship between man and wife (Genesis 4:1).[31] This underlying meaning of personal intimacy is carried over into the New Testament, in which we find Paul's statement in 1 Corinthians 8:3 that "if anyone loves God, this one is known by Him." This same meaning is likewise found in Galatians 4:9 as well as 2 Timothy 2:19. Interestingly enough, the latter is really a quotation of Numbers 16:5, in which the Hebrew word ידע is found. Thus, the Apostle, writing under the inspiration of the Holy Spirit, obviously saw the connection between γινώσκω, προγινώσκω, and ידע.

In writing on Romans 8:2-30, John Calvin stated:

> . . . [W]e are all lost in Adam. Unless God himself had by his election redeemed us from ruin, there would have been nothing but ruin to foresee. . . . The foreknowledge of God . . . which Paul mentions here, is not a mere knowing beforehand, as some ignorant people imagine in their stupid way. It is rather the act of adoption, by which God has always distinguished his children from those who are

---

30. James Strong, *A Concise Dictionary of the Words in the Hebrew Bible* (McLean, Virginia: MacDonald Publishing Company, n.d.), page 46.

31. When the Old Testament was translated into Greek in the Third Century B.C., the resulting Septuagint specifically used γινώσκω to translate the Hebrew ידע when personal relationships were in view. The Septuagint was widely used by the Jews in the time of Christ, and was therefore the primary source of the Old Testament quotes found in the New Testament.

reprobate. . . . It follows that God's knowing the elect rests upon his own good pleasure, because he foreknew nothing outside of himself which led him to will the adoption of sons. He marked some for election according to his own good pleasure.[32]

Election and God's Sovereign Will

Another verse that can be cited in support of absolute predestination is Ephesians 1:4-5, which reads: ". . . He chose us in Him before the foundation of the world, that we should be holy and without blame before Him in love, having predestined us to adoption as sons by Jesus Christ to Himself, according to the good pleasure of His will." There is in this verse no mention whatsoever of God's foresight of faith, much less of it as the basis of election. Rather, Paul clearly stated that God's adoption of sinners as His children is solely "according to the good pleasure of his will." John Gill wrote, ". . . [T]his text proves that this eternal election of particular persons to salvation is absolute, unconditional, and irrespective of faith, holiness, good works, and perseverance, as the moving causes or conditions of it. . . ."[33]

Another passage with the same meaning is Romans 9:10-24. Paul not only explicitly denied here that "the purpose of God according to election" (verse 11) depends upon "him who wills, nor of him who runs" (verse 16) but went on to write:

---

32. John Calvin, *Commentaries on the Epistle to the Romans* (Grand Rapids, Michigan: Baker Book House, 1993), pages 317-318.

33. Gill, *Cause of God*, page 85.

Therefore He has mercy on whom He wills, and whom He wills He hardens. . . . Does not the potter have power over the clay, from the same lump to make one vessel for honor and another for dishonor? What if God, wanting to show His wrath and to make His power known, endured with much longsuffering the vessels of wrath prepared for destruction, and that He might make known the riches of His glory on the vessels of mercy, which He had prepared beforehand for glory, even us whom He called, not of the Jews only, but also of the Gentiles? (verses 18, 21-24).

Calvin referred to Romans 9:6-29 as "that memorable passage from Paul which alone ought easily to compose [settle] all controversy among sober and compliant children of God."[34] Indeed, these verses so clearly define election and reprobation in terms of unconditionality[35] that it is understandable why so few Arminians are willing to comment on them.[36]

---

34. John Calvin, *Concerning the Eternal Predestination of God* (Cambridge, England: James Clarke and Company, Ltd., 1961), 5:3.

35. This is not to suggest that, like the elect, the reprobate are equally undeserving of how God deals with them. There is nothing in the elect which warrants God's favor; they are, with the reprobate, equally deserving of His wrath for their sins. However, it is God's sovereign prerogative to choose some and reject others, and therein lies the unconditionality spoken of in this passage.

36. John Wesley, however, felt compelled to respond to Calvin's usage of Romans 9:6-29 in support of unconditional predestination by writing, "Whatever that scripture proves, it never can prove this doctrine [predestination]; whatever its true meaning be, this cannot be its true meaning. . . . But this I know, better it were to say it had no sense at all, than to say it had such a sense as this. . . . No scripture can mean that God is not love, or that his mercy is not over all his works; that is, what-

The Arminian's insistence that election is contingent upon God's foresight of faith also directly contradicts such passages as 1 Peter 1:2, which clearly teaches that believers were foreknown and chosen *for*, not *because of*, obedience to Jesus Christ. Ephesians 2:10 likewise states that Christians were saved to *do* good works, not *because of* them.[37] Certainly,

---

ever it prove beside, no scripture can prove predestination" (*Works of Wesley*, Volume VII, page 383). Wesley was so confirmed in his rejection of unconditional predestination that he preferred to view certain passages of Scripture as nonsensical rather than admit they clearly taught the doctrine. As is the case with most Arminians, Wesley's emotions became the hermeneutical rule for his interpretation of the Bible and his understanding of God Himself, thus proving true Calvin's observation: "Like water gushing forth from a large and copious spring, immense crowds of gods have issued from the human mind, every man giving himself full license, and devising some peculiar form of divinity, to meet his own views" (*Institutes*, Book I, Chapter 5:12).

37. It is ironic that Calvinists are often accused of succumbing to legalism when it is actually the Arminian who is guilty of teaching such a false system of salvation. Spurgeon wrote:

> Do you not see at once that this is legality – that this is hanging our salvation upon our work – that this is making our eternal life to depend on something we do? Nay, the doctrine of justification itself, as preached by an Arminian, is nothing but the doctrine of salvation by works, after all; for he always thinks faith is a work of the creature, and a condition of his acceptance. It is as false to say that man is saved by faith as a work, as that he is saved by the deeds of the Law. We are saved by faith as the gift of God, and as the first token of His eternal favour to us; but it is not faith as our work that saves, otherwise we are saved by works, and not by grace at all (quoted by Murray, *Forgotten Spurgeon*, pages 80-81).

Calvin likewise wrote, "Unless these points are put beyond controversy, though we may ever and anon repeat like parrots that we are justified by faith, we shall never hold the true doctrine of justification.

the exercise of faith in Christ is itself a "good work" (John 6:28-29), and since Scripture declares, as we have already seen, that "it is the gift of God" (Ephesians 2:8), it would be erroneous to assert that God did not sovereignly choose those whom He was pleased to save:

> "You did not choose Me, but I chose you and appointed you that you should go and bear fruit, and that your fruit should remain. . . .
> "If the world hates you, you know that it hated Me before it hated you. If you were of the world, the world would love its own. Yet because you are not of the world, but I chose you out of the world, therefore the world hates you" (John 15:16, 18-19).

> But we are bound to give thanks to God always for you, brethren beloved by the Lord, because God from the beginning chose you for salvation through sanctification by the Spirit and belief in the truth, to which He called you by our gospel, for the obtaining of the glory of our Lord Jesus Christ (2 Thessalonians 2:13-14).

The Logical Absurdity of "Corporate Election"

Another argument used to support the Arminian rejection of God's sovereign election of certain men for salvation is the doctrine of *corporate election*, or *eternal ecclesiastical election*. Adherents to this doctrine claim that God has "elected" a corporate body of people to salvation (the Church), but inclusion in that group is left open to each in-

---

tion. It is not a whit better to be secretly seduced from the alone foundation of salvation than to be openly driven from it" (*Calvin's Tracts* [Edinburgh: Calvin Translation Society, 1851], Volume III, page 254).

dividual's own choice. Consequently, all of mankind has been "elected" to salvation in Christ, but only those who actually place their faith in Him have fulfilled their election.

This view was held by German theologian Karl Barth, who was accused by many of his contemporaries of teaching a form of universalism. Barth interpreted such passages as 2 Corinthians 5:19, which speaks of the reconciliation of "the world" in Christ, to mean that the Savior's death obliterated the barrier of sin which separated every man from God, and that all are now equal recipients of God's grace and love. Most Lutheran theologians today would heartily agree with Barth in asserting that "in Christ Jesus, God has declared the entire world of sinners forgiven."[38] Thus, modern Lutheranism categorically denies the biblical teaching of a particular redemption, which will be discussed in the next chapter.

For those Arminians who admit that God's foreknowledge cannot be interpreted biblically in terms of mere foresight, the idea of a corporate election offers yet another opportunity to escape the "horrible decree" of predestination. However, corporate election is just as indefensible from a scriptural, as well as a logical, standpoint.

At best, the concept of corporate election is a half-truth. It is obvious that God predestined the Church, or the Body of Christ, to be seated in heavenly places and to partake of His eternal blessing as His own chosen people. Indeed, no Calvinist would ever attempt to deny such a proposal. However, the logic of Pinnock and others who hold to this view is shown to be hopelessly flawed when they conclude

---

38. Don Matzat, *Christ Esteem* (Eugene, Oregon: Harvest House Publishers, 1990), page 88.

that "in this way, election, far from arbitrarily excluding anybody, encompasses them all potentially."[39] What, we might ask in response, is the Church but the gathering together of real *individuals?* The Body of Christ is certainly not some amorphous entity made up of "potential" members whom God in His divine ignorance hoped some day would enter therein by an act of their own free will, but a vibrant organism made up of actual believers and servants of Christ.

In attempting to avoid the obvious problem of the Arminian definition of foreknowledge as it relates to individuals, the proponents of corporate election are nevertheless faced with the very same problem. As we have already seen, foreknowledge in the biblical sense of the word clearly implies personal intimacy. Since the Bible declares that God foreknew His Church, how can it possibly be asserted that He did not really *know* those who would ultimately be included in that body?[40] Clearly, His foreknowledge and election was of individuals (Acts 13:48; Revelation 13:8), and therefore corporate election is not only biblically disproved, but is also shown to be a logical absurdity.

Does Calvinism Really Discourage Evangelism?

The Arminian charge against Calvinism at this point is that the system does not encourage, and even *discourages,*

---

39. Pinnock, "From Augustine to Arminius," page 19.

40. Pinnock stated, ". . . [T]he idea of corporate election would have had the further advantage of not requiring absolute divine omniscience. . . ." (*ibid.,* page 20). It is difficult to understand how Pinnock could possibly see the rank denial of an essential attribute of God as an "advantage," but at least he rightly viewed such a conclusion as a necessity of his premise. See Appendix Three.

evangelism. John Wesley, referred to by Charles Spurgeon as the "prince of Arminians,"[41] spoke for all anti-Calvinists when he wrote:

> Call it therefore by whatever name you please, Election, Preterition, Predestination, or Reprobation, it comes in the end to the same thing. The sense of all is plainly this: By virtue of an eternal, unchangeable, irresistible decree of God, one part of mankind are infallibly saved and the rest infallibly damned; it being impossible that any of the former should be damned, or that any of the latter should be saved. But if this be so, then is all preaching in vain.[42]

However, when taking into consideration that the means of evangelism is as essential to God's decree as the end of the salvation of the elect, this objection is shown to be very weak. Preaching the Gospel is just as much a duty of the obedient Christian as is living a holy life. Believers are commanded by Scripture to share their faith with others, for it is through the message of the cross that men are saved: "For 'whoever calls on the name of the Lord shall be saved.' How then shall they call on Him in whom they have not believed? And how shall they believe in Him of whom they have not heard? And how shall they hear without a preacher?. . . So then faith comes by hearing, and hearing by the word of God" (Romans 10:13-14, 17).

The same Christ who instructed His followers to "go into all the world and preach the gospel to every creature" (Mark 16:15), also said in John 14:21, "He who has My com-

---

41. Spurgeon, *Autobiography*, Volume I, page 173.

42. John Wesley, "Free Grace," *The Works of the Reverend John Wesley* (New York: B. Waugh and T. Mason, 1833), Volume I, page 483.

mandments and keeps them, it is he who loves Me." The truly regenerate heart will be compelled to evangelize others because it is driven to obey its Master: "For if I preach the gospel, I have nothing to boast of, for necessity is laid upon me; yes, woe is me if I do not preach the gospel! For if I do this willingly, I have a reward; but if against my will, I have been entrusted with a stewardship" (1 Corinthians 9:16-17). Actually, it is Arminian theology that does injustice to biblical evangelism by insisting that God needs the cooperation of fallen men in order to save them. The Calvinist minister, on the other hand, while understanding that only the elect will be saved, and this solely by God's sovereign power and grace, nevertheless does not know who these individuals are, and therefore preaches the Gospel message to everyone without discrimination.[43] In the presentation of the Gospel, he is aware that, while it is erroneous to declare that Christ died for all, it is nevertheless true that each and every man is guilty before God for his sins and will be eternally damned for them if he does not come to Christ seeking forgiveness. Thus, while it *is* true that all men need to, and in fact, have a duty to repent, it is *not* true, in light of the fallen condition of the human heart, that all men are desirous and therefore *capable* of repentance.

---

43. Of this notion, William MacDonald wrote, "It is ultimately a faithless question, arising out of false presuppositions about God, to ask, '*Am I elect?*'" ("The Biblical Doctrine of Election," *Grace of God/Will of Man*, page 225; emphasis in original). MacDonald's complaint is unwarranted, for this is simply not a question that will ever be asked by the reprobate who has no regard for either God or his own soul. This question would also not be asked by the believer who truly understands God grace, for without divine intervention, he, like the reprobate, would not even give it a second thought.

Not only does the Arminian once again misunderstand Calvinism here, he also shows himself to be ignorant of much of Church history. If indeed Calvinism discourages evangelism, as is claimed, then one might justifiably ask how it is that nearly all of the greatest evangelists since the Protestant Reformation have been either five-point Calvinists, or extremely inconsistent Arminians. As we have seen, Charles Spurgeon, whose devotional writings are widely read by Calvinists and Arminians alike, and whose preaching resulted, by God's grace, in thousands of converts, referred to Calvinism as "the gospel, and nothing else," and viewed his own ministry as a "daily labour to revive the *old* doctrines of Gill, Owen, Calvin, Augustine, and *Christ*" (emphasis in original).[44] Jonathan Edwards was also a staunch Calvinist, as was renowned Puritan John Owen, perhaps the greatest expositor of the doctrine of limited atonement, and the eminent Baptist preacher John Bunyan, whose *Pilgrim's Progress* is still received as a classic work without equal by, not only Arminians, but the secular world as well. Even such men as John and Charles Wesley, though Arminian in ideology, proved to be virtual Calvinists in practice, not only many times in their evangelism, but in the composition of some of the most beloved hymns of the Church.

The following comments of Spurgeon are conclusive:

> The greatest missionaries that have ever lived have believed in God's choice of them; and instead of this doctrine leading to inaction, it has ever been an irresistible motivating power, and it will be so again. It was the secret energy of the Reformation. It is because free grace has been

---

44. Spurgeon, quoted by Murray, *Forgotten Spurgeon*, page 58.

put into the background that we have seen so little done in many places. It is in God's hand the great force which can stir the church of God to its utmost depth. It may not work superficial revivals, but for deep work it is invaluable. Side by side with the blood of Christ, it is the world's hope.[45]

45. Spurgeon, quoted by Murray, *ibid.*, page 113.

CHAPTER THREE
Limited Atonement

A Brief Definition of Limited Atonement

Perhaps the most maligned, yet least understood, doctrine of Calvinism is *limited atonement*.[1] Simply defined, this doctrine states that since God the Father chose of His own pleasure and will those who would be saved, the Son, who came only to do the will of His Father, gave His life as a ransom for these individuals and for none others. In other words, the cross had the very specific design of providing atonement for God's elect, thereby reconciling them to divine favor, but it accomplished nothing in regard to those not chosen for salvation.

---

1. The terms *particular redemption* or *definite atonement* would perhaps better illustrate the doctrine than *limited atonement*. The latter tends to a misunderstanding that Calvinism teaches an atonement which is somehow limited in its power to save rather than limited in its extent, while the former two more precisely describe an atonement which, though indeed limited in extent, is nevertheless quite definite in what it was intended to accomplish and in what it actually did accomplish for particular individuals. However, since the Calvinistic system is commonly represented by the acronym T-U-L-I-P – limited atonement, of course, being represented by the L – the latter term will be utilized throughout this book.

The doctrine of limited atonement is rejected by modern Lutherans, as well as by Dispensationalists and others who attempt to identify themselves as "moderate Calvinists." Of course, to the Arminian, who believes that God does not sovereignly and eternally elect individuals to salvation, thereby reprobating the rest to eternal damnation, the teaching that Christ did not die for all men without exception is highly objectionable and will often elicit such responses as the following:

> First, the doctrine of limited atonement is *logically contradictory* to the clear teaching of passage after passage of Scripture. . . . Secondly, it is *theologically repugnant*, for it misunderstands the nature of God and of man. . . . Third, it is *philosophically deficient*, for the very existence of reason, or the ability to know, shows that man is capable of choice. Some doctrine of human freedom is essential to any meaningful theory of human responsibility (emphasis in original).[2]

It is a common Arminian claim that John Calvin himself did not hold to the doctrine of limited atonement, for he did not devote as much time to it as he did to predestination, election, reprobation, and the other so-called distinctives of his system. For example, Donald M. Lake wrote:

> What is important . . . is the fact that the issue of limited atonement does not appear in Calvin, but belongs to second generation Calvinists. . . . [I]t must be emphasized that the question of the extent of Christ's redemptive grace had received no real examination by Calvin. For him the question is rather: does God save all men? That is a question of election, not of the atonement. This fact is all the more

---

2. Miethe, "Universal Power," page 92.

surprising, since Calvin is one of the Church's greatest exegetical theologians.[3]

Lake's observation is only partially correct. It is true that Calvin did not specifically address this issue at any great length in his writings. However, this is likely because he did not see the need to do so. If God sovereignly distinguished between those who would be saved and those who would not be saved, why would He then send His Son into the world to die in the place of and purchase the salvation of those who would never be saved?[4] In his monumental treatise on limited atonement entitled, *The Death of Death in the Death of Christ*, the great Puritan theologian John Owen wrote, ". . . [H]ow strange it seems that Christ should be the

---

3. Donald M. Lake, "He Died For All: The Universal Dimensions of the Atonement," in Clark H. Pinnock (editor), *Grace Unlimited* (Minneapolis, Minnesota: Bethany House Publishers, 1975), page 33.

4. There are, however, passages in Calvin's writings from which the doctrine of limited atonement may be inferred. For example, regarding the subject of election, he wrote: "The covenant of life is not preached equally to all. . . . This diversity displays the unsearchable depth of the divine judgment, and is without doubt subordinate to God's purpose of eternal election. But . . . it is plainly owing to the mere pleasure of God that salvation is spontaneously offered to some, while others have no access to it. . . ." (*Institutes*, Book III, Chapter XXI:1). Without a doubt, Calvin recognized that the Gospel was the simple preaching of the cross (1 Corinthians 2:2), and yet he clearly believed that God has not made this message available equally to all men. While acknowledging the doctrine of election in Calvin's writings, Lake would have the eminent "exegetical theologian" introducing inconsistencies into the work of the other two Persons of the Godhead: i.e. the Son dies for some the Father did not elect, and the Spirit fails to regenerate all for whom the Son died.

Saviour of them who are never saved, to whom He never gives grace to believe, for whom He denies to intercede."[5] Reformed theologian Loraine Boettner likewise stated:

> That a man's accomplishments oftentimes do not measure up to his expectations is due to his lack of foresight or to his lack of ability to accomplish what he purposes. But even a man does not expect what he knows will not be accomplished. . . . They do but deceive themselves who, admitting God's foreknowledge, say that Christ died for all men; for what is that but to attribute folly to Him whose ways are perfect? To represent God as earnestly striving to do what He knows He will not do is to represent Him as acting foolishly.[6]

J. I. Packer was correct in pointing out that the "five points of Calvinism" are so closely connected to one another that to deny even one of them is to deny all five.[7] Consequently, there really is no such thing as a "four-point Calvinist," for when carefully questioned, it will be discovered that he, either knowingly or unknowingly, rejects the other points by redefining them. If Christ's death was for all men without exception, then all men must have the opportunity to be saved. Since all men are not ultimately saved, they must have chosen to reject God's invitation. This is simply Arminianism in a rather thin disguise, for it denies the total depravity and inability of humanity, God's unconditional election of men, the effectual calling of the Spirit, and,

---

5. Owen, *Death of Death*, page 79.

6. Loraine Boettner, *Studies in Theology* (Nutley, New Jersey: Presbyterian and Reformed Publishing Company, 1980), page 317.

7. Packer, "Introductory Essay," page 6.

if consistent, the certainty of the final perseverance of the elect.

Belief in a universal atonement also requires a rejection of the omniscience and omnipotence of God. Firstly, He could not have really known who would eventually be saved if He anticipated and thus provided for the salvation of all; and secondly, He lacked the power to actually save all for whom Christ died. Thus, the entire system of Calvinism, and indeed the most essential doctrines of the Christian faith, can be said to stand or fall upon the doctrine of limited atonement.

The Effects of Presupposition on Interpretation

> There are a number of biblical texts that suggest that Christ died for all mankind, and an unprejudiced exegesis would take these texts at their face value. . . . Are there grounds for believing that, were it not for the prior acceptance of the theory of election . . . we should interpret the statements of universal atonement literally?[8]

It cannot be denied that everyone, Arminian and Calvinist alike, invariably approaches the Scriptures with at least some degree of presupposition. However, this is not to say that presuppositions are, in and of themselves, necessarily wrong. Indeed, there is a vast difference between *biblical* presuppositions and *unbiblical* presuppositions. For example, the doctrine of the Trinity is one example of a biblical presupposition, despite the fact that it is nowhere explicitly defined in the Bible. Since the Christian knows from innumer-

---

8. I. Howard Marshall, "Universal Atonement and Grace in the Pastoral Epistles," *Grace of God/Will of Man*, pages 52-53.

able passages of Scripture that there is only one God, when presented with other passages which speak of three Persons who each bear the name and exhibit the characteristics of Deity, he will attempt to interpret them in light of his presuppositional belief in one God. This is not an incorrect hermeneutical method, and is, in fact, responsible for the formation of many orthodox tenets of the Christian faith.

On the other hand, one example of an unbiblical presupposition is the assumption that, as a man, our Lord could have committed sin. Such an erroneous idea arises from the presupposition that true humanness necessarily includes a propensity for sin. It may be granted that the Bible itself never explicitly states that Christ could not have sinned. It does, however, clearly state that God is entirely incapable of sin. Thus, when operating from the biblical presupposition that Christ was both God and Man, we must conclude that, as such, He was incapable of sin. Consequently, those passages that would seem to indicate otherwise must be interpreted in such a manner as to do justice to the presupposition.

Howard Marshall was quite correct in pointing out in the above quote that the presuppositions which Calvinists bring to the Scriptures greatly influence their interpretation thereof. However, Arminians do the very same thing, though their presuppositions are obviously quite different from those of the Calvinist. This is why members of both theological camps will often use the very same verses or passages of Scripture against each other. What needs to be done is not to decry presuppositions as such, but to determine which is more correct in view of the overall theme of the Bible, and to interpret any troublesome passages in that light.

Alleged Proof Texts for Universal Atonement

Arminians invariably have a stockpile of "proof texts," most often completely removed from their proper context, to which they will appeal in defense of the alleged universality of the atonement. For example, John 3:16, perhaps one of the most quoted salvific texts, tells us that "God so loved the world that He gave His only begotten Son." In John 6:33, Christ described Himself as "He who comes down from heaven and gives life to the world." In 1 John 2:2, we read that Christ "is the propitiation for our sins, and not for ours only but also for the whole world." The Apostle Paul is also claimed to have had in mind a universal application of Christ's redemptive work when he wrote that "God was in Christ reconciling the world to Himself, not imputing their trespasses to them" (2 Corinthians 5:19). The Arminian will invariably go on and on quoting such passages as these to prove that the extent of the atonement was unlimited.

It is a basic tenet of biblical hermenuetics that Scripture must interpret Scripture, and this within the context of the culture in which it was written. It is fallacious to attempt to impose modern cultural ideas, terminology, or sociological trends onto the biblical text. Such an approach to reading the Bible can often result in passages being so distorted by the unbiblical presuppositions of the reader that virtually all of their original intent is lost.

When we use the Bible as its own interpreter, the word *world* can be best defined as those whom God chose and loved "out of every tribe and tongue and people and nation" (Revelation 5:9). It is helpful to remember that, with the exception of the books written by Luke, the New Testament, like the Old, was the product of Hebrew authorship. The Jews as a whole had an exaggerated view of their role as God's chosen people, and believed that only those of Hebrew descent could ever experience God's favor. As a result, Gentiles were looked upon with great disdain.

This attitude was so much a part of Jewish culture in the days of the Apostles and the early Church that many of the Jewish converts to Christianity had difficulty accepting the fact that "God has also granted to the Gentiles repentance to life" (Acts 11:18). Even the Apostle Peter was forced to change his way of thinking in this area when God sent him to the home of Cornelius, a Roman centurion, to baptize him and his household into the faith (Acts 10). Consequently, it was necessary to educate the Jewish believers that God's will was that both Jews and Gentiles alike would become members of one Body, and that ethnic origins were no longer a valid reason for excluding any man from fellowship among God's people. This was the theme of Paul's letter to the Gentile congregation at Ephesus:

> Therefore remember that you, once Gentiles in the flesh – who are called Uncircumcision by what is called the Circumcision made in the flesh by hands – that at that time you were without Christ, being aliens from the commonwealth of Israel and strangers from the covenants of promise, having no hope and without God in the world. But now in Christ Jesus you who once were far off have been brought near by the blood of Christ. For He Himself is our peace, who has made both one, and has broken down the middle wall of separation, having abolished in His flesh the enmity, that is, the law of commandments contained in ordinances, so as to create in Himself one new man from

the two, thus making peace, and that He might reconcile them both to God in one body through the cross, thereby putting to death the enmity (Ephesians 2:11-16).

Indeed, there is nothing in the Scriptures, when read in this light, that would suggest that God loved and extended His mercy to every person of every tribe, language, and nation, for if such were the case, He certainly would have decreed that all would be saved. Instead, God has proven that He "shows no partiality, but in every nation whoever fears Him and works righteousness is accepted by Him" (Acts 10:34-35). He does not condemn anyone on the basis of ethnicity, but wills "that all [Jew and Gentile] should come to repentance" (2 Peter 3:9).

Does "World" Always Mean Every Man?

Lest the foregoing information be dismissed as "personal interpretation," let us examine the usage of the Greek word κόσμος (*kósmos* – *world*) in other contexts to determine if universality is always, or even often, the necessary interpretation.

In John 1:10, the Apostle stated that though "the world was made through Him [Christ] . . . the world did not know Him." In John 12:19, the Pharisees observed that "the world has gone after Him." In 1 John 5:19, the Apostle wrote that "the whole world lies under the sway of the wicked one." Finally, in Revelation 12:9, the Devil is described as he "who deceives the whole world." These verses were all written by the same man who wrote John 3:16, and yet, if the usage of κόσμος is here given the same meaning which Arminians insist must be applied there, they would be rendered mean-

ingless. Clearly, there were those who did in fact acknowledge the true identity of Christ. Nathaniel, the disciple,
recognized Him as "the Son of God . . . [and] the King of
Israel" (John 1:49). Peter's great confession was that He was
"the Christ, the Son of the living God" (Matthew 16:16). To
this list may be added the Magi (Matthew 2:2), John the
Baptist (John 1:29), Elizabeth (Luke 1:43), Simeon (Luke 2:30),
Anna (Luke 2:38), as well as all professing believers, including Arminians, since that time. The Pharisees' statement that
"the world has gone after Him" also cannot possibly be
understood universally, since they themselves, as well as
Israel in general, utterly rejected Jesus as their Messiah. In
fact, Jesus Himself condemned them by declaring, "You are
not willing to come to Me that you may have life" (John
5:40). Finally, John's words that "the whole world lies under
the sway of the wicked one" and that Satan "deceives the
whole world" cannot mean everyone on the planet since
Christians have turned "from darkness to light, and from
the power of Satan to God" (Acts 26:18) and thus "are not
ignorant of his devices" (2 Corinthians 2:11).

Likewise, the usage of "all" or "all men" in Scripture
can be shown to be limited by the context in which these
words appear. For example, Christ warned His followers
in Matthew 10:22 that "all men" would hate them on account
of His Name. Matthew 21:26 states that "all count John as
a prophet." In John 11:48, the Sanhedrin reasoned that if
Jesus were allowed to continue performing miracles, "all
men" would believe in Him, leaving the Jewish temple and
their own religious status vulnerable to Roman desecration.
Again, if taken in the Arminian sense of "all men without
exception," these verses would be meaningless. The disciples

were not in fact hated by all men without exception, for there were many who gladly received their message and joined their ranks (Acts 2:41). In fact, in Acts 2:47, the disciples are described as "having favor with all the people." If nothing else, Christ's early followers were not hated by their own fellow believers. Clearly, then, the "all men" of whom Christ spoke were a specific group of people – namely, those who would not repent and believe. All men without exception did not hold John as a prophet, for, by their own admission, the chief priests and the Jewish elders did not (Matthew 21:25). Finally, the Sanhedrin did not fear that all men without exception would believe in Christ, for they certainly did not intend to, nor did they entertain the possibility that the Romans would either.

Calvinism and the Common Call of the Gospel

Having thus established that κόσμος does not always, and, in fact, rarely means "all men on the planet," and that "all men" does not always refer to "all men without exception," the Arminian is forced to admit that the Calvinist position in regards to the atoning work of Christ is at least a possibility, if not completely consistent with the Scriptures. However, for the sake of argument, let us now examine the verses most frequently quoted in favor of God's alleged universal saving will, beginning with the following:

Come to Me, all you who labor and are heavy laden, and I will give you rest (Matthew 11:28).

And the Spirit and the bride say, "Come!" And let him who hears say, "Come!" And let him who thirsts come.

Whoever desires, let him take the water of life freely
(Revelation 22:17).

It is difficult to understand just how the Arminian can
appeal to such verses as these to support the doctrine of an
unlimited atonement, for the audience to which the invitations are given is clearly restricted to those "who labor and
are heavy laden" and to "him who thirsts." Such can only
be those who have experienced the heavy burden of their
own sins and have thus thirsted for the righteousness of
Christ. Indeed, as Jesus Himself stated, "Those who are well
have no need of a physician, but those who are sick"
(Matthew 9:12). It was for this reason that He did not come
"to call the righteous, but sinners, to repentance" (Matthew
9:13).

The Arminian labors under the false assumption that
men everywhere are desperately seeking God, and need only
to be presented with the "good news" that He loves them
and "has a wonderful plan for their lives." However, according to the Bible, this simply is not the case at all. For example,
in John 3:19, we find God's condemnation of the men of the
world because they "loved darkness rather than light,
because their deeds were evil." In Paul's polemic against
the entire human race in Romans 3:10-18, he wrote not only
that "there is none who understands; there is none who seeks
after God" (verse 11), but that "there is no fear of God before
their eyes" (verse 18). This observation prompted him to
later write, "For to be carnally minded is death, but to be
spiritually minded is life and peace. Because the carnal mind
is enmity against God; for it is not subject to the law of God,
nor indeed can be. So then, those who are in the flesh cannot
please God" (Romans 8:6-8).

The Pharisees and the teachers of the Law were not then included in Christ's invitation simply because they did not view themselves as needy of salvation, and therefore were neither "heavy laden" nor "thirsty" (cf. Luke 18:9-14). Thus, His accusation against them was justified: "But you are not willing to come to Me that you may have life" (John 5:40). Since we read in Romans 8:6 that "to be spiritually minded [led by the Spirit] is life and peace," we can only conclude that Christ's offer of eternal life and spiritual rest applied only to those whom the Holy Spirit had effectually prepared to respond favorably to Him – the elect (John 10:25-27).

Paul's Comparison of Adam and Christ

> [T]hrough one man sin entered the world, and death through sin, and thus death spread to all men, because all sinned. . . . But the free gift is not like the offense. For if by the one man's offense many died, much more the grace of God and the gift by the grace of the one Man, Jesus Christ, abounded to many. . . . Therefore, as through one man's offense judgment came to all men, resulting in condemnation, even so through one Man's righteous act the free gift came to all men, resulting in justification of life. For as by one man's disobedience many were made sinners, so also by one Man's obedience many will be made righteous (Romans 5:12, 15, 18-19).

Arminians will point to this passage and argue that since the effect of Adam's fall was universal, the effect of Christ's atoning death must also be universal. For example, Donald Lake wrote, "Then as one man's trespass led to condemnation for all men, so one man's act of righteousness leads to acquittal and life for all men."[9] The reader should notice that Lake's paraphrase of Romans 5:18 is, in reality, a perversion of the actual text, inserting the phrases "led to" and "leads to" where they were not originally used. Perhaps Lake was aware of what most Arminians have missed in their interpretation of this passage: Adam's fall did not *potentially* condemn his descendants, but *actually* plunged the entire human race into sin and estrangement from God. To make a direct and unqualified parallel between the damning effects of Adam's fall and the propitiating effects of Christ's sacrifice would result in the teaching that all men are actually saved since, like condemnation, justification refers to an actual legal pronouncement, not merely a possibility. In the words of John Gill, "A judge, when he either acquits or condemns, he does not offer the sentence of justification or condemnation, but pronounces either. So God, when he justifies, he does not offer justification to men, but pronounces them righteous, through the righteousness of his Son; and when Christ procured justification, it was not an offer of it, but the blessing thereof."[10]

It is apparent therefore that Paul was here comparing Adam and Christ as the representative heads of their respective families – two groups that are nevertheless clearly distinguished from one another. Just as sin was imputed to the physical posterity of Adam, so was righteousness imputed to the spiritual posterity of Christ. In other words, verse 18 is merely stating that "all men" who are "in Christ" are justified, just as all who are "in Adam" are condemned

---

9. Lake, "He Died For All," page 78.

10. Gill, *Cause of God*, page 37.

(1 Corinthians 15:22). The Arminian insistence upon absolute equality between the two groups, and a common identity, utterly destroys the contrast which Paul intended to make. To the Calvinist, however, who realizes that "the gift" is "not like the offense," this passage does not create any such difficulty.

Does God Will That Every Man Be Saved?

> For this is good and acceptable in the sight of God our Savior, who desires all men to be saved and to come to the knowledge of the truth (1 Timothy 2:3-4).

It cannot be disputed that coming to "the knowledge of the truth" is inseparable from salvation.[11] The question can be raised, however, as to whether or not "the knowledge of the truth" is the *means* by which salvation is attained or is the *result* of salvation. The truth does indeed set men free, as Christ promised in John 8:32, but does Scripture necessarily teach that the knowledge thereof is the catalyst which sets its power into motion? In other words, does the Bible indicate that the truth is effective in and of itself apart from a sovereign work of God in the human heart?

In John 14:6, Jesus said, "I am the way, the truth, and the life. No one comes to the Father except through Me." To come to "the knowledge of the truth" is to receive spiritual enlightenment regarding one's spiritual condition and to recognize Jesus Christ alone as the solution to what

---

11. It is evident that Scripture makes a clear distinction between saving knowledge and mere intellectual assent. For example, in James 2:19 we read that "the demons believe – and tremble."

is an exclusively spiritual problem. Keeping in mind that 1 Corinthians 2:14 restricts such spiritual knowledge to those to whom the Spirit of God has come in regenerating power, it is the bold assertion of the Calvinist that only those actually purchased and redeemed by Christ are able to, and ultimately will, recognize Him as Savior and Lord.

It is significant that Paul did not describe God as desiring that all men *first* come to the knowledge of the truth and *then* be saved, which is how the average Arminian would interpret 1 Timothy 2:3-4, but he instead reversed the order, placing a knowledge of the truth subsequent to actual salvation. The Lord Jesus Himself did this same thing in John 8:31 by making discipleship a previous condition to being set free by the knowledge of the truth.

In Matthew 11:25-26, we also read the following: "At that time Jesus answered and said, 'I thank You, Father, Lord of heaven and earth, that You have hidden these things from the wise and prudent and have revealed them to babes. Even so, Father, for so it seemed good in Your sight.'" Here we learn from the Savior's own lips that God has deliberately restricted a knowledge of "these things" (the identity and work of His Son) to only a few – those who have become as "a little child" by adoption into God's family (Mark 10:15). This is entirely consistent with the Calvinist's claim that only those whom God the Father has sovereignly elected, for whom the Son has effectively died, and whom the Spirit has irresistibly drawn will ever believe. The internal sentence structure of the verse notwithstanding, the Arminian insistence based on 1 Timothy 2:3-4 that God's salvific will is universal in scope, simply cannot stand in light of Matthew 11:25, especially when cross-referenced to 1 Corinthians 1:26.

If God indeed wills that all men know His Son and thus be saved, then He certainly would not have purposefully withheld such vital information from the vast majority of men throughout history, as He clearly has done (Matthew 7:14).

The Arminian interpretation of 1 Timothy 2:3-4 also cannot be true without reducing God to a schizophrenic deity whose actions do not correspond to his own will. According to the Scriptures, however, there exists no such discrepancy between what God wills and what God actually does.[12] For example, in Job 23:13, we read that God does exactly "whatever His soul desires." In Isaiah 14:24, God said of Himself, "Surely, as I have thought, so it shall come to pass, and as I have purposed, so it shall stand." Thus, we see the effectual nature of God's will in general. However, the same may be said of His will in relation to mankind in particular. In Daniel 4:35, the exiled Babylonian king Nebuchadnezzar testified that God "does according to His will in the army of heaven and among the inhabitants of the earth," and according to Proverbs 16:4, Acts 13:22, Revela-

---

12. Oddly enough, John Wesley himself criticized the notion that God and His will could be separated, stating that the latter could not be considered apart from what we know about God Himself: "It seems then, that the whole difficulty arises from considering God's will as distinct from God: otherwise it vanishes away. For none can doubt but God is the cause of the law of God. But the will of God is God himself. It is God considered as willing thus or thus" ("The Origin, Nature, Property, and Use of the Law," *Works of Wesley*, Volume V, pages 440-441). Granted, Wesley made the above statement with God's mercy and love in mind. In other words, God's will could never be anything but merciful and loving. However, we also know from Scripture that God is omnipotent. Using Wesley's logic, may we not then say that God's will itself is nothing less than all-powerful and thus efficacious?

tion 17:17, and other similar passages, the actions of both the godly and the ungodly are orchestrated by God's hand to fulfill His will. On numerous occasions, Paul declared himself to be "an apostle of Jesus Christ by the will of God" (2 Corinthians 1:1; Ephesians 1:1; Colossians 1:1; 2 Timothy 1:1), and he readily acknowledged that his sufferings, as well as that of all believers, were a result of God's will (Philippians 2:29) – a fact later confirmed by Peter when he wrote of "those who suffer according to the will of God" (1 Peter 4:19). Finally, in Ephesians 1:11, we are told that God "works all things according to the counsel of His will." There is no indication given in this verse, or anywhere else in the Bible, that would suggest that "all things" may be interpreted so as to exclude salvation, for this too is made a reality in the lives of His elect according to His "good pleasure" (Philippians 2:13).

John Gill wrote regarding 1 Timothy 2:4:

> . . . [T]he salvation which God here wills that all men should enjoy, is not a mere possibility of salvation for all, nor putting all men into a salvable state, nor an offer of salvation to all, nor a proposal of sufficient means of it to all in his Word; but a real, certain, and actual salvation, which he has determined they shall have, has provided and secured in the covenant of his grace, sent his Son into this world to effect, which is fully effected by him.[13]

So, then, who are the "all men" of whom the Apostle speaks in this verse? The answer is apparent from its context: "Therefore I exhort first of all that supplications, prayers,

---

13. Gill, *Cause of God*, page 49.

intercessions, and giving of thanks be made for all men, for kings and all who are in authority, that we may lead a quiet and peaceable life in all godliness and reverence" (1 Timothy 2:1-2). Clearly, "all men" is to be understood as *all kinds* of men – God does not restrict salvation to those of either a lowly or a lofty estate, but has extended His grace to men of every station of life.

How God is the "Saviour of All Men"

> For to this end we both labor and suffer reproach, because we trust in the living God, who is the Savior of all men, especially of those who believe (1 Timothy 4:10).

In dealing with this verse, it is important to once again remind ourselves not to impose modern cultural thought or language upon the biblical text, but rather attempt to understand it through the eyes of its original readers. To contemporary Evangelicals, the title of *Savior* has very definite connotations of either God or Christ as the spiritual source of eternal life. However, in the Hebrew culture, from which the Christian Church arose, this meaning was not at all times stressed. The Hebrew word יׁשע (*yasha* – *to save* or *deliver*) literally means "to open wide" or "to make safe,"[14] and was used when speaking of the preservation of physical life. The following Old Testament passages are given here as examples of this usage:

> Then David spoke to the LORD the words of this song, on the day when the LORD had delivered him from the hand

---

14. Strong, *Hebrew Dictionary*, page 53.

of all his enemies, and from the hand of Saul. And he said: "The LORD is my rock and my fortress and my deliverer; the God of my strength, in whom I will trust; my shield and the horn of my salvation, my stronghold and my refuge; my Savior, You save me from violence (2 Samuel 22:1-3).

In that day there will be an altar to the LORD in the midst of the land of Egypt, and a pillar to the LORD at its border. And it will be for a sign and for a witness to the LORD of hosts in the land of Egypt; for they will cry to the LORD because of the oppressors, and He will send them a Savior and a Mighty One, and He will deliver them (Isaiah 19:19-20).

Men such as Moses, Joshua, Samson, David, and others, were thus saviors in this sense because of their heroic deeds in behalf of Israel. Ultimately, however, Yahweh was viewed by the Israelites as the only Savior (Isaiah 43:11), particularly in light of their deliverance from Egyptian bondage, which prompted the Psalmist to speak of "God their Savior" (Psalm 106:21). The primarily temporal meaning behind this specific usage of יֵשַׁע is undeniable, particularly when this verse is read in context with the statement, "then they despised the pleasant land; they did not believe His word," only a few verses later (verse 24). Such would completely discount any underlying reference to spiritual regeneration.

This concept of Yahweh as the Preserver and Deliverer of mankind can also be found in the New Testament with the Greek word σωτήρ (sōter), albeit with the often added implication that "He will save His people from their sins" (Matthew 1:21). In Hebrews 1:3, Christ is described as "upholding all things by the word of His power." In his Mars

Hill discourse, the Apostle Paul informed his audience that it was in God that "we live and move and have our being" (Acts 17:28). Even Jesus Himself testified that His Father "makes His sun rise on the evil and on the good, and sends rain on the just and on the unjust" (Matthew 5:45). Such an idea has traditionally been known in Reformed circles as *common grace*, or *divine kindness*.[15] Louis Berkhof described this doctrine as follows:

> This is a grace which is communal, does not pardon nor purify human nature, and does not effect the salvation of sinners. It curbs the destructive power of sin, maintains in a measure the moral order of the universe, thus making an orderly life possible, distributes in varying degrees gifts and talents among men, promotes the development of science and art, and showers untold blessing upon the children of men.[16]

In this way, God is indeed the "Savior [preserver or sustainer] of all men," though His paternal care is obviously more focused upon those whom He has rescued from eternal damnation (*particular grace*). Even W. E. Vine, who himself was an Arminian, listed this as one of the possible meanings of σωτήρ in his widely used *Expository Dictionary of New Testament Words*, specifically using 1 Timothy 4:10 as one example.[17]

It has been suggested by some scholars that the Greek

15. John Calvin, *Harmony of the Evangelists* (Grand Rapids, Michigan: Baker Book House, 1993), Volume I, page 307; *Institutes*, Book III, Chapter 24:17.

16. Berkhof, *Systematic Theology*, page 434.

17. Vine, *Expository Dictionary*, page 1004.

word μάλιστα (*málista*), which is usually translated "especially," as in 1 Timothy 4:10, may have the alternate meaning of "namely."[18] If this is true, it provides yet another reason to reject the Arminian interpretation of this verse as a proclamation of God's universal saving will, for the verse would then tell us that God "is the Savior of all men, namely those that believe." Either way, "all men" must refer to men out of all nations, or men of every station in life, rather than all men in general. The alternative is that all men are actually saved by God's grace, which experience itself tells us is not the case.

Is Saving Grace Given to All Men?

> For the grace of God that brings salvation has appeared to all men . . . . (Titus 2:11)

The same interpretation of "all men" as *all kinds*, or *classes*, of men must again be applied to this verse, for "all men without exception" would not fit the context. First of all, Paul opened this epistle to Titus by referring to himself as "a bondservant of God and an apostle of Jesus Christ, according to the faith of God's elect and the acknowledgment of the truth which accords with godliness" (Titus 1:1). We have already sufficiently established that when speaking of "God's elect," the authors of Scripture had in mind specific individuals whom He has sovereignly chosen for salvation. Furthermore, as we have seen, "acknowledgment of the truth" is possible only for these individuals, since they alone,

---

18. T. C. Skeat, "Especially the Parchments: A Note on 2 Timothy 4:13," *Journal of Theological Studies*, ns 30 (1979), pages 173-177.

by the indwelling Holy Spirit, are able to comprehend the truth. Consequently, there can be no doubt that in writing to Titus, Paul had in mind a very clear distinction between the elect and the reprobate.

If salvation, as used in Titus 2:11, is to be understood as the gift of eternal life, as indeed it should be in light of Titus 1:2, then the interpretation of "all men" in the Arminian sense must again be rejected because it is described in this verse as what the grace of God *actually*, not *potentially*, brings. This thought is continued in verse 14 and later in Titus 3:4-7, and may also be cross-referenced to 2 Timothy 1:9-10: "[God] who has saved us and called us with a holy calling, not according to our works, but according to His own purpose and grace which was given to us in Christ Jesus before time began, but has now been revealed by the appearing of our Savior Jesus Christ, who has abolished death and brought life and immortality to light through the gospel."

Clearly, then, the appearance of "the kindness and the love of God our Savior" (Titus 3:4) resulted in the salvation of those to whom it appeared. Again, no mere offer is here described, but rather a definite and completed act of divine mercy. If this is to be applied to all men without exception, then all men without exception have therefore been "justified by His grace" and have become "heirs according to the hope of eternal life" (Titus 3:7), which, of course, very few Arminians would accept.

Did Christ Die For False Prophets?

But there were also false prophets among the people, even as there will be false teachers among you, who will secretly bring in destructive heresies, even denying the Lord who bought them, and bring on themselves swift destruction (2 Peter 2:1).

At face value, the above verse is perhaps one of the most difficult to reconcile with the doctrine of limited atonement, and is therefore a favorite proof text of Arminian universality. However, this difficulty exists only in the English translation, and disappears quickly when the original language is examined. First of all, it should be noted that this verse makes no reference to either Christ or the redemption of the cross. The Greek title δεσπότης (despótais – sovereign) which appears here, is applied exclusively to the Father in such passages as Luke 2:29 and Acts 4:24. Since δεσπότης indicates "absolute and unlimited authority,"[19] it is never used in reference to Christ, who, as the begotten Son of God, is in subjection to the Father.[20]

---

19. James Strong, *A Concise Dictionary of the Words in the Greek New Testament* (Maclean, Virginia: MacDonald Publishing Company, n.d.), page 36.

20. Some of the newer translations, such as the New International Version, render Jude 4 so as to imply that both δεσπότης and κύριος (kúrios) are applicable to Christ (i.e. "Jesus Christ our only Sovereign and Lord"). Both the older and newer King James Versions, however, differ from these by making a clear distinction in this verse between the Father and the Son: "the only Lord God, and our Lord Jesus Christ." The discrepancy between these renditions arises from a slight variation in the different manuscripts. In the Textus Receptus, which is the basis of the KJV and the NKJV, we find the definite article τόν (ton – the) inserted after the conjunction καί (kai – and), while in the Nestle-Aland text from which most of the modern versions were translated, this article is absent. The former of the two is likely the more accurate, particularly since it better reflects the economic subordinational theology of the New Testament (1 Corinthians 15:28).

It might be helpful to note that Peter was an apostle to the Jews, and therefore his epistles should be read from the Jewish perspective. Again, the Hebrew understanding of God as "Savior" primarily referred to His mighty acts of deliverance in behalf of Israel's physical well-being. As such, He "redeemed" them from slavery in Egypt and took them as His own people. On a more intimate level, Israel is even referred to many times in the Old Testament as the spouse of the Lord God (Ezekiel 16), and reference is often made to the bride price which was paid for her. In either case, God's "purchase" of Israel signified that she was His possession and therefore was obligated to obey and worship Him. For example, we read in Deuteronomy 32:6, "Do you thus deal with the LORD, O foolish and unwise people? Is He not your Father, who bought you? Has He not made you and established you?" Since it is obvious that the Father did not shed His blood on Calvary, in what way, then, did He "buy" the false prophets? Peter's predominantly Jewish audience would have immediately recognized the parallel being drawn between unfaithful Israel and the false teachers of the Church. Though they were "married" to Yahweh, the Israelites repeatedly turned their backs on Him and committed spiritual adultery by worshipping the idols of the nations around them. Likewise, the false teachers in the New Testament Church made a public profession of faith in and allegiance to God through Christ, and yet they had turned "from the holy commandment delivered to them" (2 Peter 2:21). Thus, to "deny" God was to apostatize into idolatry and to demonstrate the reprobation of one's heart: "They profess to know God, but in works they deny Him, being abominable, disobedient, and disqualified for every good work" (Titus 1:16).

Again, the question must be asked, Why would the Father send the Son to die for the sins of those whom He had no intention of saving? Just as was the case in Deuteronomy 13:1-5, the infiltration of false prophets into the Church was ordained by God to test the faithfulness of His people. Like Judas, these "ravenous wolves" in "sheep's clothing" (Matthew 7:15) will "honor [God] with their lips" (Matthew 15:8) and even perform "many wonders" (Matthew 7:22), but they are motivated by satanic influence and unregenerate hearts.

As we have seen, Scripture teaches that God "foreknew" (had personal intimacy with) those whom He had elected for eternal life, and yet Christ's clear declaration to these men will be that He *never* knew them (Matthew 7:23). Thus, they had not possessed salvation at one time through faith in the redemption of the cross, and then had turned away from it. They simply were never saved to begin with. Peter specifically stated that "their judgment has not been idle, and their destruction does not slumber" (2 Peter 2:3). The Greek text here literally reads, "the judgment of old is not idle" (τὺ κρίμα ἔκπαλαι οὐκ ἀργεῖ – *to krima ékpalai ouk argei*). This is an obvious reference to a pretemporal reprobation to damnation, the outworkings of which Peter saw as currently manifest. This thought is also clear in Peter's first epistle, when he wrote of the disobedience of some "to which they also were appointed" (1 Peter 2:8), and in Jude 4 when Scripture speaks of "certain men [who] have crept in unnoticed, who long ago were marked out for this condemnation." These men, by deceiving others, willingly fulfill their role in God's plan, and thus are deserving of their ultimate fate. As "slaves of corruption" (2 Peter 2:19), they certainly have never been given the grace to repent and believe, and therefore for them "is reserved the blackness of darkness forever" (verse 17). Since there is no indication that either Christ or the Apostles ever prayed for such men as these, and no command is given for us to do so, it would be absurd to suggest that the redemption of the cross equally applies to false prophets and heretics as to the elect.

All Men Were Not Redeemed By Christ

Though the above thesis does not deal with every biblical passage or verse that has ever been cited in support of the Arminian doctrine of a universal atonement, such should be sufficient to prove false the allegations that Calvinists approach the salvation texts with unbiblical pre-suppositions and misinterpret them accordingly. To the contrary, there are many Scriptures that, when read without an Arminian bias, clearly indicate that Christ's death was in behalf of a specific group of people. For example, Jesus saved "His people from their sins" (Matthew 1:21), while those who are not His people are left to die in their sins (John 8:24). He came "to give His life a ransom for many" (Matthew 20:28; Mark 10:45) – "a great multitude which no one could number, of all nations, tribes, peoples, and tongues" (Revelation 7:9) – but he did not die for all men who ever lived or will live on the earth. He gave "His life for the sheep" (John 10:11), but He rejects the "goats" (Matthew 25:41) who are "not of [His] sheep" (John 10:26). "Christ also loved the church and gave Himself for her" (Ephesians 5:25), and "He purchased [her] with His own blood" (Acts 20:28). It is therefore "His people," "the sheep," and "the church" for whom Christ prayed in John 17:6-10, and for none others:

> "I have manifested Your name to the men whom You have given Me out of the world. They were Yours, You gave them to Me, and they have kept Your word. Now they have known that all things which You have given Me are from You. For I have given to them the words which You have given Me; and they have received them, and have known surely that I came forth from You; and they have believed that You sent Me. I pray for them. I do not pray for the world but for those whom You have given Me, for they are Yours. And all Mine are Yours, and Yours are Mine, and I am glorified in them."[21]

Furthermore, in Luke 19:10 we read, "For the Son of Man has come to seek and to save that which was lost." Such was the Incarnation twofold in its purpose: Christ came to seek *and* to save. The seeking cannot be divorced from the saving, as if the one act could be accomplished and the other left undone. Even more specifically, we must understand that Christ came to ransom, or to make atonement for, His "sheep" by the shedding of His blood. Now, the concept of ransom is very explicitly described in Scripture as the actual acquiring of that which was sought and paid for. The Greek word λύτρον (*lútron*) also carries the meaning of "a loosing," with reference to a former state of debt, bondage, etc.[22] For exam-

---

21. Lest it be argued that this passage refers specifically to the eleven disciples, it should be remembered that these men — the "little flock" of Luke 12:32 — were the nucleus of the New Testament Church (Ephesians 2:20). Christ's prayer was therefore in behalf of, not only those present at that time, but also for those who would believe in Him throughout the ages (John 17:20).

22. Vine, *Expository Dictionary*, page 929.

ple, in Exodus 21:30, if a man's bull killed another man, he was required to pay a ransom price to purchase back his innocence, thereby "loosing" himself from bloodguiltiness. In Leviticus 25:24, the Israelites were commanded to "ransom" the land, thereby "loosing" it from the former owner, and in Leviticus 19:20, this same concept of acquiring and "loosing" is applied to the ransom of slaves.

This last illustration is most significant in light of the ransom provided for the elect by Christ. If the elect are truly purchased "with the precious blood of Christ" (1 Peter 1:19), then they have actually become His "purchased possession" (Ephesians 1:14) and are therefore distinguished from the world as His "own special people" (1 Peter 2:9). Hence, they no longer belong to themselves, but as the slaves of Christ, they must relinquish all things, including their own wills, unto His service (1 Corinthians 6:19-20; 2 Corinthians 5:15). Simply stated, a slave has no right to choose whether or not he will serve in the capacity for which he was purchased. Furthermore, those whom Christ purchased have been "loosed" from their former state of bondage to sin and death, and have been granted the blessings of eternal life instead. To limit this gift to those who accept it is to say that the blood of Christ was a down payment which merely guaranteed that all men would have the *opportunity* to be saved rather than that some would *actually* be saved.

The concept of atonement is also very definite in the Scriptures. Under the Levitical system of the Old Covenant, the barrier between God and man was represented by the thick veil which hung in the temple between the Holy of Holies and the outer court. Every year on the Day of Atonement, the high priest entered the inner chamber to make a symbolic atonement for the people with the blood of a lamb "without blemish" (Exodus 12:5). Under the New Covenant, however, Christ, who is both High Priest and sacrificial Lamb, entered the heavenly Temple of which the earthly temple was but a type and shadow, and forever tore in two the veil of sin separating the elect from God's presence (Luke 23:45):

> And as they were eating, Jesus took bread, blessed and broke it, and gave it to the disciples and said, "Take, eat; this is My body." Then He took the cup, and gave thanks, and gave it to them, saying, "Drink from it, all of you" (Matthew 26:26-27).

> Neither by the blood of goats and calves, but by his own blood he entered in once into the holy place, having obtained eternal redemption for us. . . . And for this reason He is the Mediator of the new covenant, by means of death, for the redemption of the transgressions under the first covenant, that those who are called may receive the promise of the eternal inheritance. . . . [B]ut now, once at the end of the ages, He has appeared to put away sin by the sacrifice of Himself. And as it is appointed for men to die once, but after this the judgment, so Christ was offered once to bear the sins of many. To those who eagerly wait for Him He will appear a second time, apart from sin, for salvation (Hebrews 9:12, 15, 26-28).

Christ's Work Was Completed on the Cross

In light of the Scriptures discussed above, it is the firm conviction of the Calvinist that the Atonement was a reality, not merely a wishful thought. In the Reformed system, God's redemptive plan was brought to completion, the sins of His chosen ones were actually remitted, and the Body of Christ (the Church) was literally purchased with His blood. However, to the Arminian, who insists on a democratic view of salvation in which sinful man has ultimate veto power over the decrees of Almighty God, this cannot be true:

> Christ's death on behalf of the race evidently did not automatically secure for anyone an actual reconciled relationship with God, but *made it possible* for people to enter into such a relationship by faith (emphasis added).[23]

> The atonement is that aspect of the work of Christ, particularly his death, that *makes possible* the restoration of fellowship between God and humankind. . . .
> God's plan, the scheme of redemption, was to *offer* salvation through the very life and death of his Only Begotten One (emphasis added).[24]

This insistence on a potential redemption simply cannot be supported from Scripture. In addition to Ephesians 2:5, which tells us that God "made us alive together with Christ" when "we were dead in trespasses," we also have the Apostle's testimony in Colossians 1:21-22: "And you, who once were alienated and enemies in your mind by wicked works, yet now He has reconciled in the body of His flesh through death, to present you holy, and blameless, and above reproach in His sight." Arminians would, of course, argue that God "made us alive" and "reconciled" us at the moment we "exercised faith" in Christ. The Apostle Paul, however, clearly stated in Galatians 2:20 that he had been

23. Pinnock, "From Augustine to Arminius," page 23.
24. Miethe, "Universal Power," page 72.

"crucified with Christ," and that, just as the whole race died with Adam, so all of the elect were made alive through Christ's death and resurrection. In other words, not only was our redemption purchased on the cross nearly two thousand years ago, but our Advocate immediately took His place before the great heavenly Bar to secure our pardon. The elect, "not yet being born, nor having done any good or evil," were released from the prison of eternal condemnation, "that the purpose of God according to election might stand, not of works but of Him who calls" (Romans 9:11).

This doctrine of a completed, pre-birth redemption, which utterly demolishes the Arminian emphasis on human autonomy and personal salvific choice, can also be seen clearly in Hebrews 10:11-14: "And every priest stands ministering daily and offering repeatedly the same sacrifices, which can never take away sins. But this Man, after He had offered one sacrifice for sins forever, sat down at the right hand of God, from that time waiting till His enemies are made His footstool. For by one offering He has perfected forever those who are being sanctified." The phrase "has perfected forever" is in the aorist tense, signifying past completed action, not continuing action in the present. The question now facing the Arminian is whether Christ succeeded or failed in His mission to save sinners. There is absolutely no room for mere possibilities here; either He accomplished the work for which He was sent into the world by the Father, or He did not.[25] If His work *was* completed,

---

25. John Owen's illustration may be helpful here:

> God imposed his wrath due unto, and Christ underwent the pains of hell for, either all the sins of all men, or all the sins of some men, or some sins of all men. If the last, some sins of all men, then have

then Arminianism is false; if His work was *not* completed, then Christ was an imposter and those who follow Him "are of all men the most pitiable" (1 Corinthians 15:19). Fortunately, such a dilemma does not face the Calvinist who reads the Bible as a whole, for no clearer declaration of Christ's completed mission could be hoped for than His own final words on Calvary: "It is finished" (John 19:30).[26]

The following words of Charles Spurgeon are conclusive:

> We are often told that we limit the atonement of Christ, because we say that Christ has not made a satisfaction for all men, or all men would be saved. Now, our reply to this

---

all men some sins to answer for, and so shall no man be saved. . . . If the second, that is it which we affirm, that Christ in their stead and room suffered for all the sins of all the elect in the world. If the first, why, then, are not all freed from the punishment of all their sins? You will say, "Because of their unbelief; they will not believe." But this unbelief, is it a sin, or not? If not, why should they be punished for it? If it be, then Christ underwent the punishment due to it, or not. If so, then why must that hinder them more than their other sins for which he died from partaking of the fruit of his death? If he did not, then did he not die for all of their sins (*Death of Death*, pages 61-62).

26. The single Greek word here is τετέλεσται (*telélestai*), the root word of which is τελέω (*teléō*) which is translated "to end, to finish" (Revelation 20:3, 5, 7), "to fulfill, to accomplish" (Luke 2:39; James 2:8), or "to pay" (Matthew 17:24). It was in this last context that the word was stamped on tax bills and other financial documents, signifying that the bearer's debt had been "paid in full" (Matthew 17:24; Romans 13:6). Finally, τετέλεσται is in the perfect tense, which denotes past action with results continuing into the present. Jesus did not *potentially* pay the sin debt for an undetermined people, but *actually* "wiped out the handwriting of the requirements that was against us, which was contrary to us. And He has taken it out of the way, having nailed it to the cross" (Colossians 2:14).

is, that, on the other hand, our opponents limit it: we do not. The Arminians say, Christ died for all men. Ask them what they mean by it. Did Christ die so as to secure the salvation of men? They say, "No, certainly not." We ask them the next question – Did Christ die so as to secure the salvation of any man in particular? They answer, "No." They are obliged to admit this, if they are consistent. They say, "No, Christ has died that any man may be saved if" – and then follow certain conditions of salvation. Now, who is it that limits the death of Christ? Why, you. You say that Christ did not die so as infallibly to secure the salvation of anybody. We beg your pardon, when you say we limit Christ's death; we say, "No, my dear sir, it is you that do it." We say Christ so died that He infallibly secured the salvation of a multitude that no man can number, who through Christ's death not only may be saved, but are saved, must be saved and cannot by any possibility run the hazard of being anything but saved. You are welcome to your atonement; you may keep it. We will never renounce ours for the sake of it.[27]

---

27. Spurgeon, quoted by Packer, "Introductory Essay," page 14.

CHAPTER FOUR

Irresistible Grace

Common Misconceptions About the Doctrine

Irresistible grace, the fourth point of Calvinism, is so closely related to the first, that in the original Canons of Dordt, the two points were actually combined into one.[1] The Westminster Confession's explanation of this doctrine cannot be improved upon:

> All those whom God hath predestinated unto life, and those only, He is pleased, in His appointed and accepted time, effectually to call, by His Word and Spirit, out of that state of sin and death, in which they are by nature, to grace and salvation, by Jesus Christ; enlightening their minds spiritually and savingly to understand the things of God, taking away their heart of stone, and giving them a heart of flesh; renewing their wills, and, by His almighty power, determining them to that which is good, and effectually drawing them to Jesus Christ: yet so, as they come most freely, being made willing by His grace.[2]

---

1. See Appendix One.
2. Westminster Confession of Faith, Section X:1.

This doctrine is often misunderstood and grossly mis-represented by its opponents to render God a tyrannical usurper of the free will of men. As we have seen previously, Arminians invariably view the God of Reformed theology as an arbitrary monster who created some men for the sole purpose of damning them without regard to their actions, and, likewise, forces the rest to submit to Him whether they are willing to do so or not. One critic of Calvinism de-nounced irresistible grace as "spiritual rape" which "over-throws the whole plan of salvation."[3] The comments of Dr. Norman Geisler, an outspoken Arminian writer, are similar:

> If free choices were not considered at all when God made the list of the elect, then irresistible grace on the unwilling follows. Humans would have no say in their salvation. Accordingly, the fact that some (even all) do not choose to love, worship, and serve God will make no difference whatsoever to God. He will simply dou-ble-whammy them with his irresistible power and bring them screaming and kicking into his kingdom against their will. . . .
>
> Irresistible grace (?) on the unwilling is a violation of free choice. For true love is persuasive but never coercive. There can be no shotgun weddings in heaven. . . .
>
> Irresistible force used by God on his free creatures would be a violation of both the charity of God and the dignity of humans. God is love. True love never forces itself on anyone. Forced love is rape, and God is not a divine rapist![4]

---

3. Vance, *Other Side of Calvinism*, page 307.

4. Dr. Norman Geisler, "God Knows All Things," in Randall Basinger and David Basinger (editors), *Predestination and Free Will* (Downers

With such a mental picture as this, it is no wonder that the Arminian struggles so vehemently against the doctrine before us. However, Calvinism does not teach that men are dragged "screaming and kicking" into heaven, but that they come willingly: "It is drawing, which denotes not a force upon the will, but a change wrought in the will. A new bias is given to the soul, by which it inclines to God."[5]

Again, it should be remembered that the will and desires of a man are dictated by his own nature. Men are not forced to sin against their will; they sin, and will continue to do so, because sin is inherent to their fallenness. Likewise, God does not force anyone to come to Christ and believe against their will; the elect come because the ruling principle of their inward nature has been transformed from sinfulness to righteousness. Hence, the former reject Christ because they want to (John 5:40), and the latter accept Him because they also want to (Psalm 110:3): "Man's freedom consists in his being able to act freely (i.e. not under compulsion or constraint applied from without) in a manner consistent with his will; but fallen man's will is depraved, and from this depravity he can be rescued only by the grace of God in Christ."[6]

Grove, Illinois: InterVarsity Press, 1986), pages 68-69. The question that immediately comes to mind is, Since when is rape properly defined as "forced love"? Rape is a brutal act of dominance over another man or woman and has nothing at all to do with love. This is why the Mosaic law prescribed the death penalty for the convicted rapist (Deuteronomy 22:25). Geisler's remark is an insensitive insult to anyone who has been victimized by this terrible crime.

5. Matthew Henry, *Commentary on the Whole Bible* (Grand Rapids, Michigan: Zondervan Publishing House, 1961), page 1540.

6. Sell, *Great Debate*, page 17.

How Fallen Men Resist the Holy Spirit

> God desires all to be saved, but all are not saved. Jesus longed to gather the Jews as a mother hen gathers her chicks, but they were not willing. God did not want them to resist the Spirit, but they did resist him. . . . Contrary to Calvin and Augustine, God's will is not always done.[7]

The logical conclusion of the Arminian belief that man, of his own volition, may choose to receive Christ, is that he may also choose to reject the Holy Spirit's calling unto salvation. However, as a false premise must produce a false conclusion, the Arminian myth of free will in fallen man results in the erroneous idea that God's alleged will to save all men without exception can be thwarted by human unbelief. Passages such as Acts 7:51 are invariably relied upon to dispute irresistible grace: "You stiff-necked and uncircumcised in heart and ears! You always resist the Holy Spirit; as your fathers did, so do you." Commenting on this verse, Laurence Vance triumphantly stated, "How miserable is the Calvinist tortured by this portion of Scripture!"[8] However, if this verse is returned to its proper context, it becomes clear that it does not "torture" the Calvinist in the slightest. The speaker, Stephen, here rebuked the Jewish leaders for placing

---

7. Pinnock, "Response to John Feinburg," in Basinger and Basinger, *Predestination and Free Will*, page 58. As do most Arminians, Pinnock completely missed the point of Matthew 23:37, which says nothing at all about the Jewish people resisting God's will for their salvation. Instead, Christ was addressing the Jewish *leaders,* who sought to prevent the people's entrance into God's Kingdom by keeping them under a legal bondage (Matthew 23:13).

8. Vance, *Other Side of Calvinism*, page 299.

him on trial for testifying to the truth. These were the same men with whom Jesus Himself had contended not long before: "Which of you convicts Me of sin? And if I tell the truth, why do you not believe Me? He who is of God hears God's words; therefore you do not hear, because you are not of God. . . . But you do not believe, because you are not of My sheep, as I said to you" (John 8:46-47, 10:26).

The Jews did not believe the words of either Christ or Stephen because, like their forefathers, they had not been regenerated by the Holy Spirit, and were therefore "uncircumcised" in their hearts and ears. Though outwardly religious, they were nevertheless "enmity against God" (Romans 8:7) and, according to our Lord's words in Matthew 23:27-28, they were spiritually dead. Of course they resisted the testimony of the Holy Spirit through the preaching of the Gospel. Not having been granted repentance and new life, these reprobates were left to their own wicked nature and therefore could do nothing else: "He has blinded their eyes and hardened their heart, lest they see with their eyes, and understand with their heart, and turn, and I would heal them" (John 12:40; cf. 2 Corinthians 4:4).

The point of Acts 7:51 is that the Jews were obstinate towards the outward witness of the Holy Spirit through the preaching of His ministers, not that they were resistant to the inward drawing power of God's grace. Though the external call of the Gospel for all men to repent and believe is the same, the internal application of this message so as to affect a saving change within the human heart depends entirely upon a sovereign act of God's grace:

> I will sprinkle clean water on you, and you shall be
> clean from all your uncleannesses, and from all your idols

I will cleanse you. And I will give you a new heart, and a new spirit I will put within you. And I will remove the heart of stone from your flesh and give you a heart of flesh. And I will put my Spirit within you, and cause you to walk in my statutes and be careful to obey my rules (Ezekiel 36:25-27).

No true Christian has ever complained that they have been "spiritually raped" or otherwise violated by God's sovereign choice of them in eternity or by the effectual grace which He bestows upon them in time. Quite the contrary, the heart that understands this truth will be filled with overwhelming gratitude for the abundant mercy of God: "When iniquities prevail against me, you atone for our transgressions. Blessed is the one you choose and bring near, to dwell in your courts! We shall be satisfied with the goodness of your house, the holiness of your temple!" (Psalm 65:3-4).

The Secret Will and the Revealed Will of God

The Calvinist cannot conceive of God desiring something to take place which never does, but God can. . . . That God has a directive or imperative will that can be rejected by man we now examine further, and consequently see the utter fallacy of the Calvinist position. . . .

How many Christians from the first century until the present day have either committed fornication or been unthankful? [referring to 1 Thessalonians 4:3, 5:18] How many thousands? Is there a Calvinist who would dare say that fornication and unthankfulness were God's will and part of his decree? Then how else would you account for man ignoring and rejecting God's will other than the idea that sometimes God's will is ideal and commanded yet unrealized and disobeyed?[9]

In dealing with such an argument as this, the very important distinction should be understood between the secret, eternal will of God, and His revealed, temporal will. That God has an eternal purpose in that which He decreed before time is abundantly clear from Scripture (Ephesians 1:11). It is this will that is said to be immutable and free from contingency (Isaiah 46:10). However, there is also the prescriptive will of God that has been revealed to man in the form of commands, the Ten Commandments being the best example. When God told the Israelites, "You shall have no other gods before Me. You shall not make for yourself a carved image. . . . You shall not take the name of the LORD your God in vain. . . ." (Deuteronomy 5:7, 8, 11), etc., He was revealing the behavior which is pleasing to Him and that which is not, as well as defining man's duty to act accordingly. It is obvious that these commandments were not included in that which God "predestined to take place" (Acts 4:28), for the nation of Israel constantly transgressed the statutes of the Mosaic code.

The Bible likewise tells us that God "now commands all men everywhere to repent" (Acts 17:30). It is therefore the duty of sinful men to respond favorably to the Gospel when presented to them, and yet God's eternal election of His people is certainly not frustrated when all do not do so. While the secret will of God in saving only those whom He has chosen is unknown to us and therefore not part of the Gospel message, His revealed will that all must repent is nevertheless preached to everyone without distinction in

---

9. Vance, *ibid.*, pages 306-307.

order that men may be justly punished for their rejection of it. In other words, no man may appeal to God's eternal reprobation of himself as justification for his continued disobedience because such a decree is not known to him. What *is* known is God's demand of obedience from His creatures, and thus, in rebelling against Him and despising His Word, the unbeliever is justly condemned by his own sin:

> A master requires of his servant to do what he commands, not to accomplish what he intends, which perhaps he never discovered unto him; nay, the commands of superiors are not always signs that the commander will have the things commanded actually performed, but only that they who are subjects to this command shall be obliged to obedience, as far as the sense of it doth extend.[10]

The Arminian Misinterpretation of John 6:44

> No one can come to Me unless the Father who sent Me draws him; and I will raise him up at the last day (John 6:44).

This verse is perhaps the clearest proclamation of irresistible grace that anyone could possibly hope to find in the Bible. These words cannot be dismissed as the mere theological speculations of a sixteenth-century Frenchman, for upon them is the very stamp of divine authority. From the lips of the Savior Himself we learn that man is unable to come to Christ in faith unless he is first drawn by the Father.

The appearance of the Greek verb ἑλκύω (*helkúō*) in this

---

10. John Owen, "A Display of Arminianism," *The Works of John Owen, D.D.* (New York: Carter and Brothers, 1856), Volume X, page 46.

verse is very significant. Meaning to "compel with irresistible superiority,"[11] or simply "to drag,"[12] this same verb is found in John 21:6, 11 ("they were not able to draw it [their net] in because of the multitude of fish" and "Simon Peter went up and dragged the net to land, full of large fish"), Acts 16:19 ("they seized Paul and Silas and dragged them into the marketplace to the authorities"), Acts 21:30 ("the people ran together, seized Paul, and dragged him out of the temple"), James 2:6 ("Do not the rich oppress you and drag you into the courts?"), and many others. It is very clear in light of the manner in which it is used in the above verses what this word meant to the New Testament writers.

Admitting that the usual meaning of ἑλκύω is as the Calvinist insists, W. E. Vine nevertheless attempted to offer an alternate, and "less violent" definition for this verb when it is used of God's "drawing" power.[13] Other Arminians, such as Billy Graham and C.S. Lewis, agreed:

> Faith in Christ is . . . voluntary. A person cannot be coerced, bribed, or tricked into trusting Jesus. God will not force His way into your life. The Holy Spirit will do everything possible to disturb you, draw you, love you – but finally it is your personal decision. God not only gave His Son . . . He gave the Holy Spirit to draw you to the cross, but even after all this, it is your decision whether to accept God's free pardon or to continue in your lost condition.[14]

11. R. C. Sproul, *Chosen By God* (Wheaton, Illinois: Tyndale House Publishers, 1986), page 69.

12. James Strong, *A Greek Dictionary of the New Testament* (Grand Rapids, Michigan: Baker Book House, 1981), page 27.

13. Vine, *Expository Dictionary*, page 338.

14. Graham, *How to Be Born Again*, pages 193-194.

But you now see that the Irresistible and the Indisputable are the two weapons which the very nature of [God's] scheme forbids Him to use. Merely to override a human will (as His felt presence in any but the faintest and most mitigated degree would certainly do) would be for Him useless. He cannot ravish. He can only woo.[15]

Bruce Reichenbach asserted that the only power God exercises over men is that of persuasion, and that He therefore "calls, woos, cajoles, remonstrates, inspires and loves."[16] However, Reichenbach failed to explain how all this avoids the natural conclusion that God is at the mercy of the objects of His "wooing" and is thus reduced to a helpless beggar.

Many Arminians have used Christ's words in John 12:32 to soften the meaning of John 6:44 to a mere "wooing": "And I, if I am lifted up from the earth, will draw all peoples to Myself." This is interpreted to mean that no man will desire to come to Christ until the Father first convinces them of His love by showing them the cross. Of course, Arminian believe that all men without exception are the objects of this gentle persuasion, which they, of their own free will, may either accept or reject. Though this "gospel" presentation is most prevalent in modern evangelism and may indeed lure thousands forward in altar calls, it is grossly unbiblical. Notwithstanding our previous discussion of "all men" in its true soteriological sense, the "wooing cross" of Arminianism is nothing more than the altar of a man-centered and

---

15. C.S. Lewis, *The Screwtape Letters* (New York: The Macmillan Company, Inc., 1961), page 38.

16. Bruce Reichenbach, "God Limits His Power," in Basinger and Basinger, *Predestination and Free Will*, page 117.

God-dishonoring message. Perhaps no better example of this can be offered than the following statement by Dr. Robert Schuller:

> Do you know what my only concern is? I don't want to drive them [non-Christians] farther away than they are. And I listen to so many preachers on religious radio stations . . . and, by golly, if I wasn't a Christian, they'd drive me farther away. I'm so afraid I'm going to drive them farther – I want to attract them. . . .
>
> If we want to win people to Jesus, we have to understand where they're at. . . . Just because it's in the Bible, doesn't mean you have to preach it. And if you do, you have to say, "Who's listening to me?"[17]

The Bible certainly does little to alleviate Schuller's fears, for it promises that the preaching of the cross will be offensive to the pride of fallen men because it lays bare the sin they refuse to face in themselves. While the preaching of the cross is a glorious thing to those whom God has chosen, it has been scorned and rejected by the vast majority of mankind throughout history. Can we honestly say then that the unregenerate heart will be attracted by the very thing which exposes his guilt and condemns him?

In light of the incapacitated state of fallen mankind, it would be accurate to state that, in and of itself, the cross saves no man. Men do not fall on their knees before the cross in repentance because it is within their power to do so, but because they are brought there by God. The "drawing" in

---

17. Robert Schuller, interviewed on "The White Horse Inn," KKLA FM (Los Angeles, California), October 31, 1992. Amazingly, Schuller later identified himself in the same interview as a "five-point Calvinist."

John 6:44, therefore, must involve an effectual act of God, for without it, the cross would be worthless:

> There is a two-fold call.
> 1. There is an outward call, which is nothing else but God's blessed tender of grace in the gospel, his parleying with sinners, when he invites them to come in and accept of mercy. Of this our Saviour speaks: "Many are called, but few chosen" (Matt. 20:16). This external call is insufficient to salvation, yet sufficient to leave men without excuse.
> 2. There is an inward call, when God wonderfully overpowers the heart, and draws the will to embrace Christ. This is, as Augustine speaks, an effectual call. God, by the outward call, blows a trumpet in the ear; by the inward call, he opens the heart, as he did the heart of Lydia (Acts 16:14). The outward call may bring men to a profession of Christ, the inward call brings them to a possession of Christ. The outward call curbs a sinner, the inward call changes him.[18]

As pointed out by Leon Morris, "There is not one instance in the New Testament of the use of this verb [ἑλκύω] where the resistance is successful."[19] Imagine what the Arminian definition of ἑλκύω would do to the reading of such passages as the aforementioned Acts 16:19 or John 21:6, 11. Surely, Paul and Silas were not "wooed" into the marketplace to be flogged, but were taken somewhat more force-

---

18. Thomas Watson, "A Divine Cordial: The Saint's Spiritual Delight," *The Writings of the Doctrinal Puritans and Divines of the Seventeenth Century* (London: Religious Tract Society, 1846), Volume V, pages 115-116.

19. Leon Morris, *The Gospel According to John* (Grand Rapids, Michigan: Wm. B. Eerdman's Publishing Company, 1971), page 371 (footnote).

fully.[20] Even more assuredly, the fish were not "wooed" onto the disciples' boat, but were caught in their nets and dragged aboard. Likewise, spiritually dead sinners are not merely entreated and enticed to come to Christ, but are actually brought to Him by the Father. A.W. Martin wrote, "In the eyes of the Calvinist sinful man stands in need, not of inducements or of assistance to save himself, but precisely of saving. He holds that Jesus Christ has come, not to advise, urge or woo, or to help a man to save himself, but to save him, to save him through the prevalent working of the Holy Spirit."[21]

God's Grace and the External Call of the Gospel

It has been suggested by some scholars that ἐλκύω may be related to αἱρέωμαι (hairéōmai), which means "to take for oneself, to prefer, [or] to choose."[22] This claim is shown to be plausible by 2 Thessalonians 2:13-14: "But we are bound to give thanks to God always for you, brethren beloved by the Lord, because God from the beginning chose you for salvation through sanctification by the Spirit and

---

20. The alert Arminian would no doubt point out this scenario as a contradiction of the Calvinists' claim that God does not in fact drag men to Himself against their will. In response, however, it should be noted that though the outcome of the arrest of Paul and Silas was not to their physical benefit, it was beneficial to their spiritual growth in that they thereby learned that God was faithful to deliver them from the hands of His enemies. It was not therefore likely that they accompanied their captors "screaming and kicking," but they went willingly, having submitted themselves to the will of their Lord and Master.

21. A. W. Martin, *The Practical Implications of Calvinism* (Edinburgh, Scotland: The Banner of Truth Trust, 1979), page 13.

22. Strong, *Greek Dictionary*, page 8.

belief in the truth, to which He called you by our gospel, for the obtaining of the glory of our Lord Jesus Christ." There are several components in this passage which require our attention. The first is God's act of choosing for Himself those whom He loved. The fact that this action is described in the aorist tense and is coupled with the phrase "from the beginning" (ἀπ' ἀρχῆς – *ap' archais*; compare John 1:1), is a clear indication that it is not merely a response to temporal conditions that must be met by its objects (such as the exercise of faith), but is an unconditional choice that God made in eternity to save some, but not others. This salvation is realized through the primary means of "sanctification by the Spirit," and through the secondary means of "belief in the truth." However, it is important to also notice that antecedent to both of these is the call of the Gospel. Thus, we see the Reformed doctrine of salvation by grace in its four necessary stages: (1) predestination, (2) the call of the Gospel, (3) the regenerating work, or "drawing," of the Spirit, and finally, (4) conversion.

Though the Gospel message of Christ's payment of the debt of sin is to be preached to all men indiscriminately, the effect of the message upon the hearer is determined by whether he is of God's elect or not. To the non-elect, indeed "those who are perishing," the message of the cross is regarded as foolishness (1 Corinthians 1:18). To the man whom God has chosen, however, the Gospel is a welcome remedy for the heavy burden of guilt and sin. Though all are equally spiritually dead in sin, and though the message that enters the ears of each man is the same, by it one heart is made alive and receptive while another remains lifeless and inactive (1 Thessalonians 1:4-5).

Jesus' parable of the "Great Banquet" in Luke 14:16-24 is an allegorical picture of this truth. In verses 16-17, we read, "A certain man gave a great supper and invited many, and sent his servant at supper time to say to those who were invited, 'Come, for all things are now ready.'" One by one, the invited guests excused themselves from participation in the feast (verses 18-20). The servant was then instructed by his master to "bring in here the poor and the maimed and the lame and the blind" (verse 21), and to "go out into the highways and hedges, and compel them to come in, that my house may be filled" (verse 23). Finally, the master of the feast concluded, "For I say to you that none of those men who were invited shall taste my supper" (verse 24).

The characters in this parable are easily identified. God the Father, who is represented by the "master," sends His "servant," the Holy Spirit, to invite all men to the "great supper" of the forgiveness of sin and everlasting life in Christ Jesus (Acts 17:30). Unregenerate men, however, excuse themselves and thereby demonstrate that they do not really want what God offers and that they are content with their own earthly possessions and pleasures (John 3:19). In contrast are "the poor and the maimed and the lame and the blind" – those who cannot afford to clothe themselves in the proper attire befitting such a social occasion (Matthew 9:13), and who can neither see the way to the supper (John 3:3) nor get to it without being carried (John 6:65). To these people (God's elect) the Spirit is sent, not merely to invite, but to compel them to come to Him. This is the true meaning of John 6:44.

Clearly, then, it is the sovereign application of the Word of God by the Holy Spirit to the hearts of men which differentiates between those who are saved and those who are lost; without this work of the Spirit, the invitation of the Gospel will always be refused. The Lord Jesus said, "All that the Father gives Me will come to Me, and the one who comes to Me I will by no means cast out" (John 6:37) and "many are called, but few are chosen" (Matthew 22:14). Simply put, those "sheep" who belong to Christ will hear and respond to the call of their Shepherd; those who do not belong to Him will not.

The Regenerating Power of the Holy Spirit

In Ephesians 1:19, the Apostle wrote of "the exceeding greatness of His power toward us who believe, according to the working of His mighty power," and in the following verse he compared the regenerating work of the Spirit upon the hearts of the elect to that which was "worked in Christ" when He was raised from the dead. The point of interest in this latter verse is the Greek verb ἐνεργέω (*energéō*), which means "to be effectual," or "to work effectually in."[23] In fact, this verb, from which we get our English verb *energize*, is never used in the Scriptures to describe work that is undergone in vain or that which is not completed.

As in Ephesians 1:19-20, ἐνεργέω is found in some instances to be connected to God's "power that works in us" (Ephesians 3:20; cf: Colossians 1:29), and in other places it is associated with His "good pleasure" (Philippians 2:13; Ephesians 1:11). Thus, we must conclude that the work which the Holy Spirit accomplishes in the hearts of the elect is both omnipotent and sovereign:

---

23. Strong, *ibid.*, page 28.

And you He made alive, who were dead in trespasses and sins, in which you once walked according to the course of this world, according to the prince of the power of the air, the spirit who now works in the sons of disobedience, among whom also we all once conducted ourselves in the lusts of our flesh, fulfilling the desires of the flesh and of the mind, and were by nature children of wrath, just as the others. But God, who is rich in mercy, because of His great love with which He loved us, even when we were dead in trespasses, made us alive together with Christ (by grace you have been saved), and raised us up together, and made us sit together in the heavenly places in Christ Jesus, that in the ages to come He might show the exceeding riches of His grace in His kindness toward us in Christ Jesus. For by grace you have been saved through faith, and that not of yourselves; it is the gift of God, not of works, lest anyone should boast (Ephesians 2:1-9).

Just as the devil, here referred to as "the prince of the power of the air," is effectually working in those who belong to him, thus producing hatred for God and behavior deserving of His wrath, so does the Holy Spirit effectually work within the elect to produce faith in God and a life which is pleasing to Him (Galatians 5:19-24). This is not the pathetic "wooing" of Arminianism, but the complete transformation of God-hating sinners into God-fearing saints. To teach that a man may frustrate a true work of God's grace through His Spirit is an arrogant lie as the following Scripture proves: "All the inhabitants of the earth are reputed as nothing; He does according to His will in the army of heaven and among the inhabitants of the earth. No one can restrain His hand or say to Him, 'What have You done?'" (Daniel 4:35).

The New Birth Typified By Resurrection

We have seen how God has "raised us up together, and made us sit together in the heavenly places in Christ Jesus." It may help to further illustrate this point with a familiar event in the earthly ministry of Christ: the raising of Lazarus from the dead. In John 11:3-4, Jesus was informed that His dear friend had become bedridden with a very serious illness, and yet He did not begin the long journey to the village of Bethany until two days later. By the time He arrived at the home of Mary and Martha, Lazarus' two sisters, the man had been dead for four days and his body had already commenced the natural process of decomposition (verse 39). Notwithstanding the inevitable stench of death, Jesus commanded that the stone to the tomb be moved aside, and then, speaking with the authority of the Son of God, He said, "Lazarus, come forth!" (verse 43) Immediately, the dead man awoke and walked out of the grave.

Though primarily demonstrating God's power to resurrect a man from physical death, this incident also may be used to illustrate His sovereign power in raising men from the deadness of sin. As we have seen, there is no greater difficulty for fallen man than to accept the fact that he is not merely spiritually sick, but completely dead. Indeed, the religions of the world are nothing more than man's attempt to improve himself or to better his inner condition by external religious works.

God's Word, on the other hand, declares that man is "four days dead" – he is a spiritual corpse that lies stinking and rotting in the darkness of the tomb of his own sin (Ephesians 2:1-2). His dead mind cannot think of life, his dead eyes cannot see life, and his dead limbs cannot raise his body from its resting place. Just as did Jesus so long ago, God also waits before He saves a man until his sins have clung to him like grave clothes and the stone of his own guilt has sealed him in the tomb of despair (James 1:13-15). It is at this point of absolute helplessness that God commands the stone to be removed through the propitiation of His Son's sacrifice (Romans 5:6), and then He floods the filthy chamber with the light of the Gospel (Ephesians 1:18). However, knowing that fresh air and sunlight (a mere outward exposure to a religious environment or to the preaching of the Word) cannot rejuvenate a corpse, God then breathes new life into the dead man and calls him from the grave (2 Corinthians 5:17). Hating the stench of his former prison, the resurrected man gladly and immediately comes forth, and presents himself to his Redeemer a willing and grateful servant (Romans 7:24-25). Although the grave clothes (symbolizing his old nature) initially still cling to his body, these God commands to be removed through the continuing sanctification of the Holy Spirit (Ephesians 5:26-27), replacing them with the fine linen of imputed righteousness (Revelation 19:7-8).

Thus, salvation does not depend upon "him who wills, nor of him who runs" – dead men can do neither – but on God "who shows mercy" (Romans 9:16). Sadly, the average Arminian church today is filled with spiritual corpses that have been exhumed from their graves by human means, arrayed in cheap linen, granted a seat at the very communion table of Christ, and yet show no evidence of life. There is no true circulation of the Word in their hearts, and so, just as the decomposition of a dead body will accelerate when it is exposed to the elements, so the outward association these people maintain with Christianity merely serves to increase their guilt before God.

The Conversion Experience of Saul of Tarsus

> For I am the least of the apostles, who am not worthy to be called an apostle, because I persecuted the church of God. But by the grace of God I am what I am, and His grace toward me was not in vain. . . . (1 Corinthians 15:9-10)

Such were the words of Paul, the mighty "apostle to the Gentiles" (Romans 11:13), which stand as a powerful testimony to the irresistible grace of God. He certainly did not see his calling and salvation as the result of his own choice, but knew that he had been "called to be an apostle of Jesus Christ through the will of God" (1 Corinthians 1:1).

Paul's conversion experience is far and above the most dramatic display in the Scriptures of God's salvific power towards His elect. In Acts 9:1-2, we are told that Paul (formerly known as Saul of Tarsus) was not only "breathing threats and murder against the disciples of the Lord," but that he was even taking them to Jerusalem to be tried and executed (cf. Acts 22:4-5). Though he led an impeccable life according to the man-made standards of the Pharisees (Philippians 3:6), these violent actions were certainly not characteristic of one who earnestly desired to believe in Christ and submit himself to His Gospel. This was a man whose heart had been blinded and hardened by his own self-righteousness to such an extent that he had become a murderer in order to maintain the facade.

Saul of Tarsus would not have been a likely candidate

for a modern "gospel" presentation. His only response to an emotional appeal to "accept Jesus" or to "try God" would have been to drag the hapless beseecher away in chains. No tear of repentance was to be found upon his cheek, no quiver of grief over sin on his lips, and yet it was to him that the Lord appeared in saving glory. The account is as follows:

> As he journeyed he came near Damascus, and suddenly a light shone around him from heaven. Then he fell to the ground, and heard a voice saying to him, "Saul, Saul, why are you persecuting Me?"
> And he said, "Who are You, Lord?"
> Then the Lord said, "I am Jesus, whom you are persecuting. It is hard for you to kick against the goads."
> So he, trembling and astonished, said, "Lord, what do You want me to do?"
> Then the Lord said to him, "Arise and go into the city, and you will be told what you must do."
> And the men who journeyed with him stood speechless, hearing a voice but seeing no one. Then Saul arose from the ground, and when his eyes were opened he saw no one. But they led him by the hand and brought him into Damascus (Acts 9:3-8).

No "wooings" are here described; no invitations offered; no regard for Saul's "free will" given. The Spirit of Christ simply acted upon the sinful heart of the man, and he was instantly regenerated. Having been knocked into the dust a wretched sinner, he rose to his feet a born-again child of God, demonstrating his inward change by rightly addressing Christ as "Lord" and obeying His command without question. Arminians such as Norman Geisler would complain that such were the "coercive" actions of a "divine rapist," but

Paul clearly viewed this momentous event in his life as the unmerited bestowal of God's gracious love upon a miserable and lost human being:

> And I thank Christ Jesus our Lord who has enabled me, because He counted me faithful, putting me into the ministry, although I was formerly a blasphemer, a persecutor, and an insolent man; but I obtained mercy because I did it ignorantly in unbelief. And the grace of our Lord was exceedingly abundant, with faith and love which are in Christ Jesus. This is a faithful saying and worthy of all acceptance, that Christ Jesus came into the world to save sinners, of whom I am chief (1 Timothy 1:12-15).

In 1 Corinthians 1:25, Paul wrote, "[T]he weakness of God is stronger than men." Clearly, the helpless "wooing" god of Arminianism was completely unknown to him, for his concept of God as the Almighty Sovereign was drawn, not only from his knowledge of the Old Testament Scriptures, but also from having personally witnessed how He could transform the "chief of sinners" into an Apostle of Christ – one who, though he once murdered Christians, would later lay down his own life in service to his Lord. The declarations of God's grace that would eventually flow from Paul's pen to comprise large portions of the New Testament bear little, if any, resemblance to the fleshly tripe that ever spews forth from Arminian pulpits as sinful men refuse to relinquish their persistent grasp on an imaginary autonomy.

The following observation of John Owen is interesting: "How do they . . . exclaim upon poor Calvin, for sometimes using the hard word 'compulsion,' describing the effectual, powerful working of the providence of God in the actions of men; but they can fasten the same term on the will of God, and no harm done!"[24] The revulsion to this doctrine that the Arminian feels, and often voices with tenacity, is conclusive evidence of the raw humanism that lies at the foundation of his theology. Man must have his "free will" at any cost, and that without divine restraints or control; and yet, no hesitation accompanies the notion that God's will is both restrained and controlled by the whimsical belief or unbelief of His own creatures. It is amazing, indeed, that the Arminian would gnash his teeth and accuse the Calvinist of blasphemy, when his own doctrines are so akin to atheism:

> [Arminianism] compels us to misunderstand the significance of the gracious invitations of Christ in the gospel . . . for we now have to read them, not as expressions of the tender patience of a mighty sovereign, but as the pathetic pleadings of impotent desire; and so the enthroned Lord is suddenly metamorphosed into a weak, futile figure tapping forlornly at the door of the human heart, which he is powerless to open. This is a shameful dishonour to the Christ of the New Testament.[25]

---

24. Owen, "Display of Arminianism," page 16.
25. Packer, "Introductory Essay," page 20.

CHAPTER FIVE

Perseverance of the Saints

The Illogical Basis of Arminian Eternal Security

The fifth and final point of the Reformed system is called the *perseverance of the saints*. This doctrine teaches that those whom God elected to salvation and whom the Son has redeemed, are likewise those whom the Spirit permanently seals and preserves. Although the name by which it is most commonly known can be misleading to those who do not really understand it, the doctrine of the final perseverance of God's elect does not focus upon what Christians must do to either earn or secure their salvation, but what they *will* do as a result of God's saving grace.[1] As in the preceding

---

1. One example of how this doctrine has been misunderstood is found in the following statement of Curtis Hutson:

> The Bible teaches, and I believe in, the eternal security of the born-again believer. The man who has trusted Jesus Christ has everlasting life and will never perish. But the security of the believer does not depend upon his perseverance.
> I do not know a single Bible verse that says anything about the saints' persevering, but there are several Bible verses that mention the fact that the saints have been preserved. Perseverance is one thing. Pre-

points, God alone deserves and receives all the glory.

It is at this point that most Arminians display the inconsistency of their personal beliefs, for though they reject God's sovereignty in salvation and elevate man's free will in choosing, popular teachers such as Charles Stanley nevertheless hold to the maxim of "once saved, always saved," or "eternal security," as it is often called.[2] In other words, the free will of man prior to salvation is vehemently defended, but is then implicitly denied by teaching that, once redeemed, the believer no longer has the free will to walk away from Christ. James White wrote:

> What is so odd about this, you ask? Well, quite simply, it makes no sense. If it was man's decision to get involved

---

servation is another. No. The saints do not persevere; they are preserved (*Why I Disagree With All Five Points of Calvinism* [Murfreesboro, Tennessee: Sword of the Lord, 1980], page 16).

The absurdity of Hutson's last statement is obvious in light of the Calvinist's conviction that believers persevere *only* because they are preserved. Neither John Calvin nor any other Reformed theologian ever claimed that the believer's security is grounded in his own perseverance. Rather, this was the position taken by John Wesley, who was a staunch opponent of Calvinism. Ironically, in his book, *The Believer's Security*, Daniel Corner faults Calvinists for teaching the very opposite of what Hutson has accused them of teaching. This sort of ignorance of Calvinism is rampant in Arminian circles.

Incidentally, some modern Reformed theologians have suggested that this doctrine be referred to as the *preservation of the saints* to avoid just such confusion (Sproul, *Chosen By God*, page 174). Indeed, this appellation would be a more accurate description of what is done to and for the elect, not what they themselves must do.

2. Charles Stanley, *Eternal Security: Can You Be Sure?* (Nashville, Tennessee: Oliver-Nelson Books, 1990).

with this whole concept of Christianity, and God was help-less to save him without his cooperation and help, then why, having entered into the bargain, can he not just up and quit? If it was my choice to join up, why isn't it my choice to get out? If man had a part in saving himself, he is highly likely to mess up somewhere down the road, and lose his salvation, or, without question, he can decide he doesn't like the living arrangements for eternity, and make arrangements on his own.[3]

Other Arminians, however, see how their system is undermined when even one point of Calvinism is given credence. For example, Daniel Corner, who mistakenly attributed the "eternal security" position to Calvinism,[4] wrote:

> Though painful to admit, you potentially can still go to hell, even if you are a Christian at this moment! To be-lieve otherwise is to be deceived about the Biblical re-cord! . . . There is a "secure position" in Christ, but it is one from which we can still "fall". . . . We must continue to follow Christ so that we will "never perish". . . .
>
> Yes, God will always do His part to protect us spiri-tually and He will never fail, but there is still free will and the human responsibility.[5]

Of course, Corner was merely calling his fellow Arminians back to the historic position of the Remonstrants:

---

3. James White, *Drawn By the Father* (Southbridge, Massachusetts: Crowne Publications, 1991), page 28.

4. Daniel Corner, *The Believer's Security: Is It Unconditional?* (Washington, Pennsylvania: Evangelical Outreach, 1995), page 1.

5. Corner, *ibid.*, pages 96-97, 105-106.

True believers can fall from true faith and fall into such sins as cannot be consistent with true and justifying faith; and not only can this happen, but it also not infrequently occurs. True believers can through their own fault fall into horrible sins and blasphemies, persevere and die in the same: and accordingly they can finally fall away and go lost.[6]

A Warning to Jewish Converts

For it is impossible for those who were once enlightened, and have tasted the heavenly gift, and have become partakers of the Holy Spirit, and have tasted the good word of God and the powers of the age to come, if they fall away, to renew them again to repentance, since they crucify again for themselves the Son of God, and put Him to an open shame (Hebrews 6:4-6).

This passage is perhaps most often quoted in opposition to the doctrine of the perseverance of the saints. As pointed out by Arthur W. Pink, "It is at this point that the hottest fights between Calvinists and Arminians have been waged."[7] In Clark Pinnock's case, these and other verses in the epistle to the Hebrews provided the initial catalyst for his eventual rejection of Calvinism in favor of Arminianism:

I held onto this view [five-point Calvinism] until about 1970, when one of the links in the chain of the tight Calvinian logic broke. It had to do with the doctrine of the perseverance of the saints, likely the weakest link in Calvinian logic, scripturally speaking. I was teaching at Trinity

---

6. Opinions of the Remonstrants, Section IV:3-4.

7. Arthur W. Pink, *An Exposition of Hebrews* (Grand Rapids, Michigan: Baker Book House, 1954), page 285.

Evangelical Divinity School at the time and attending to the doctrine particularly in the book of Hebrews. If in fact believers enjoy the kind of absolute security Calvinism had taught me they do, I found I could not make very good sense of the vigorous exhortations to persevere or the awesome warnings not to fall away from Christ, which the book addresses to Christians.[8]

Before beginning a careful exegesis of these admittedly difficult verses, we must first return the entire epistle to the historical and cultural setting in which it was penned. As its very title indicates, this epistle was originally written to first-century Hebrews who had converted to Christianity. As seen throughout, the author's intent was to explain God's "new covenant" with His people from a distinctly Hebrew perspective.

Though it certainly was God's will that His Son should die in propitiation of the sins of both Jews and Gentiles, this gracious act of love was accomplished through the means of the wicked actions of God's enemies. It should be remembered that, though Christ died upon a Roman cross, it was the religious leaders of the Jewish nation who had clamored for His death. As was the case many times in the Old Testament, the nation as a whole would have been held responsible for this horrendous crime had Jesus Himself not entreated the Father to forgive them on account of their ignorance (1 Chronicles 21:17; cf. Luke 23:34).

Among the multitudes who had gathered to witness the crucifixion and had been instigated by the Scribes and Pharisees to mock and scorn Christ, many no doubt were later to be found amongst those giving assent to Him as the

---

8. Pinnock, "From Augustine to Arminius," page 17.

Jewish Messiah. These, at least outwardly, had accepted the terms of the New Covenant, and, therefore, if they later forsook their professed faith, they had nowhere else to go but back into the apostate religious system from whence they came. In reuniting with those who crucified the Lord Jesus, they could no longer benefit from Christ's premortem intercession (Luke 23:34), since they could no longer claim ignorance. Neither could they claim the righteous status of the God-fearing Israelites who had lived before the advent of Christ, for they had actually seen with their own eyes the fulfillment of the promises which their forefathers embraced by faith without seeing (Hebrews 11:13). Thus, in returning to Judaism, they were, in a very real sense, "crucify[ing] again for themselves the Son of God." Furthermore, since the elaborate sacrificial system of the Old Covenant had been rendered theologically obsolete by the sacrifice of Christ, and actually by the later destruction of the Temple in A.D. 70, in rejecting Him as their "Paschal Lamb," these Jews no longer had any means by which their sins could be forgiven (Hebrews 9:22, 10:26-27). Consequently, as is the case with modern-day Jews who reject Christ, they were cut off from God's favor and lost forever:

> A clear and *growing* faith in heavenly things was needed to preserve Jewish Christians from relapse. To return to Judaism was to give up Christ, who had left their house "desolate." It was to fall from grace, and place themselves not only under the general curse of the Law, but that particular imprecation which had brought the guilt of Jesus' blood on the reprobate and blinded nation of His murderers (emphasis in original).[9]

---

9. A. Pridham, quoted by Pink, *Hebrews*, page 288.

Those addressed were Hebrew Christians, who, discouraged and persecuted (10:32-39), were tempted to return to Judaism. Before being received again into the synagogue they would be publicly required to make the following statements (10:29): that Jesus was not the Son of God; that His blood was rightly shed as that of a common malefactor; and that His miracles were done by the power of the evil one. All this is implied in 10:29. . . . Before their conversion they had belonged to the nation which had crucified Christ; to return to the synagogue would be to crucify to themselves the Son of God afresh and put Him to an open shame; it would be an awful sin of apostasy (Heb. 6:6); it would be like the unpardonable sin for which there is no forgiveness, because the one so hardened as to commit it cannot be "renewed unto repentance"; it would be worthy of a worse punishment than that of death (10:28); it would mean incurring the vengeance of the living God (10:30-31).[10]

Are the Enlightened Necessarily True Believers?

It is the nature of the living Word that, though originally addressed to a specific audience, it is later broadened in application by the Holy Spirit to all men within the Body of Christ. Such is clearly the case with Hebrews 6:4-6. Though Gentile members of the Church are not in danger of returning to Judaism, they are nevertheless faced with the equivalent peril of returning to the darkness of the world system. It is in this light that the Calvinist-Arminian debate is perpetuated, and is therefore the setting in which we must now examine the passage.

---

10. Myer Pearlman, *Knowing the Doctrines of the Bible* (Springfield, Missouri: Gospel Publishing House, 1937), pages 271-272.

Arminians point out that the subject cannot be other than true believers for three reasons. First, these people are spoken of as having been "once enlightened." The same Greek word φωτισθέντας (*phōtisthéntas*) is used here as in Hebrews 10:32, which speaks of apparent believers who have been "illuminated." Secondly, they are described as "partakers of the Holy Spirit." Lastly, they are said to have "tasted the heavenly gift" and "the good word of God, and the powers of the world to come." All of these phrases are taken as references to spiritual regeneration. Hence, the Arminian concludes, Christians can and some in fact do fall away and lose their salvation.[11]

---

11. Arminians who quote this verse to support the doctrine that a saint may forfeit his salvation insist that theirs is the only interpretation which considers the literal and plain sense of the text. However, most Arminians are not as literal and consistent in their reading of this passage as they would like to think. In many Arminian congregations, "backslidden" Christians are exhorted to repent of their sins and, like the prodigal son, return to the Father. Altar calls are often given, not only for rank unbelievers, but for those "who have fallen away," all the while ignoring the literal and plain words of the writer of the epistle to the Hebrews: "For it is impossible for those who were once enlightened, and have tasted the heavenly gift, and have become partakers of the Holy Spirit . . . if they fall away, to renew them again to repentance . . . ." (Hebrews 6:4, 6) If this passage does in fact teach that a true believer can lose his salvation, it also teaches that he can never get it back. Very few Arminians are willing to concede to this conclusion due to the abject terror it would inspire in the hearts of their hearers, who could never be certain just how much of God's mercy remains for them before they are eternally lost. Perhaps this is what Charles Spurgeon had in mind when he wrote, "I do not know how some people, who believe that a Christian can fall from grace, manage to be happy. It must be a very commendable thing in them to be able to get through a day without despair" (*Autobiography*, Volume 1, page 169).

We begin our rebuttal with verse 4, in which the Greek word φωτισθέντας is of primary interest. This verb most often signifies "to give light or knowledge by teaching,"[12] and is found to carry this meaning in the Septuagint translation of such Old Testament passages as Judges 13:8 ("O my Lord, please let the Man of God whom You sent come to us again and teach us what we shall do for the child who will be born") and 2 Kings 12:2 ("Jehoash did what was right in the sight of the Lord all the days in which Jehoiada the priest instructed him"). In the New Testament, φωτισθέντας may also carry the additional implication of "to manifest" or "to bring to light," as in 1 Corinthians 4:5 ("Therefore judge nothing before the time, until the Lord comes, who will both bring to light the hidden things of darkness and reveal the counsels of the hearts") and 2 Timothy 1:10 (". . . but has now been revealed by the appearing of our Savior Jesus Christ, who has abolished death and brought life and immortality to light through the gospel . . . .") The strict definition of spiritual regeneration therefore cannot be forced onto Hebrews 6:4, for, as Pink observed, "'Enlightened' here means to be instructed in the doctrine of the Gospel, so as to have a clear apprehension of it."[13]

Through the sacred truths of the Scriptures are only fully comprehended by "he who is spiritual" (1 Corinthians 2:15), it is possible for the carnal mind to achieve at least some degree of understanding with regards to God's Word, yet not have it engrafted into his heart by the Holy Spirit (James 1:21). For example, an unregenerate man can be made to un-

---

12. Pink, *Hebrews*, page 290.
13. Pink, *ibid*.

derstand intellectually that Christ paid the penalty for sin, and yet not have this fact applied to his soul so as to be transformed by it. It is also possible for someone to grasp various other doctrines of Christianity and to be entirely orthodox in his views of the Trinity, the bodily resurrection, eternal damnation, etc., and still remain unregenerate. It is to such a man that James 2:19 is addressed: "You believe that there is one God. You do well. Even the demons believe – and tremble!"

Indeed, entire nations have been "enlightened" by the public preaching of the Gospel and a prominent Christian influence, and yet it certainly would be foolish to view every citizen as truly regenerate. A survey of the moral climate of the United States alone, perhaps one of the most "Christianized" nations ever to exist, will verify this assertion. It is certain that the militant homosexual activists, the abortion rights groups, the pornographers, the drug dealers, et al., have been "enlightened" as to the commandments of God, but they respond by despising their Creator and persecuting His people: "And this is the condemnation, that the light has come into the world, and men loved darkness rather than light, because their deeds were evil" (John 3:19). It is clear that to be "enlightened" to the Gospel does not necessarily mean that a man has been inwardly changed by it. It is also interesting to note that some of the early Church fathers referred to those undergoing baptism as "illumined ones." [14] Thus, the Syriac version of Hebrews 6:4 literally reads, "Those who once have descended into baptism." Whether we under-

---

14. Justin Martyr, *First Apology*, LXI; Alexander Roberts and James Donaldon (editors), *The Ante-Nicene Fathers* (Grand Rapids, Michigan: Wm. B. Eerdman's Publishing Company, 1950), Volume I, page 159.

stand the verse in this way, or as a description of those who sit under the instruction of the Word of God, we are by no means compelled to accept the Arminian's claim that such are true believers.

The Difference Between "Tasting" and "Ingesting"

We come now to that portion of our text which speaks of those who have "tasted of the heavenly gift . . . [and] the good word of God, and the powers of the world to come." The Greek verb γεύω (*geúō – to taste*) has a variety of meanings, depending upon the context. In the majority of cases, however, γεύω has much the same connotation of a mere sampling with the tongue as our English verb to taste. Hebrews 6:4-5 is clearly one of these cases. Even some Arminians, such as W. E. Vine, have seen this "tasting" of salvation as being "different from receiving it."[15] Matthew Henry wrote, "They may taste of the heavenly gift like persons in the market, who taste of what they will not come up to the price of, and so but take a taste, and leave it."[16] This same sense can be seen in Matthew 27:34, in which polluted wine was offered to the crucified Christ, but "when He had tasted it, He would not drink." Even though Jesus did "taste death for everyone" (Hebrews 2:9),[17] and thus actually died,

---

15. Vine, *Expository Dictionary*, page 1134.

16. Henry, *Commentary*, page 1916.

17. It is unfortunate that the New King James Version renders this verse using "everyone" ("every man" in the older King James Version) for this implies a universal atonement, which, we have seen, is an unbiblical doctrine. The Greek word παντὸς (*pantós – every* or *all*) is not followed by the word ἄνθρωπος (*anthrōpos – man*). Literally, this verse reads:

this meaning of the verb cannot be applied to Hebrews 6:4-5.It is clear that the New Testament writers associated true salvation with the verbs τρώγω (*trōgō – to eat*) and πίνω (*pínō – to drink*) rather than the weaker γευω. In John 6:53, the Lord Jesus said, "Most assuredly, I say to you, unless you eat the flesh of the Son of Man and drink His blood, you have no life in you." Thus, true saving faith is not content with mere intellectual assent to the truths of the Gospel (typified by a mere taste with the tongue), but actually assimilates the principles of Christ into the heart (typified by taking food or drink into the stomach to be digested). It is to the latter group that Christ's promise is given: "Whoever eats My flesh and drinks My blood has eternal life, and I will raise him up at the last day" (John 6:54). This promise is unconditional.[18]

"... so that by [the] grace of God for every he might taste death." What then does "every" refer to? In context with the entire book of Hebrews, it must be understood as referring back to "us" (1:2), "Your companions" (1:9), "My brethren" (2:11-12), "the children whom God has given Me" (2:13), etc. In other words, Christ tasted death for every one of the elect, not for every man on earth.

18. It is true that Christ elsewhere added conditions to virtually the same promise. For example, He said, "[H]e who endures to the end will be saved" (Matthew 10:22); "[I]f you want to enter into life, keep the commandments" (Matthew 19:17); "If you keep My commandments, you will abide in My love, just as I have kept My Father's commandments and abide in His love" (John 15:10, 14), etc. However, it should be noted that the crowds to whom Christ spoke were nearly always a mixture of true believers and hypocrites. Hence, His words often served both as an assurance to the elect who would demonstrate their election by persevering, and as a warning to those of temporary and shallow faith. True Christians do not need conditions of obedience placed upon them, because the Lord has promised, "[T]his is the

In Hebrews 6:7-8, a metaphorical contrast is made between "the earth which drinks in the rain that often comes upon it, and bears herbs useful for those by whom it is cultivated," and that which "bears thorns and briers." The first land (the elect) actually ingests the nourishment of the rain (the Gospel), while the second land (the false professor) does not. Beneath a top soil that is moistened by the elements and loosened by the blade of the tiller's plow lies soil that is barren and useless.

Several other passages support this interpretation. The first of these is the parable of the sower found in Mark 4:1-20. Jesus here described four kinds of soil: the hard-packed dirt of the wayside, the sparse soil of the stony ground, the soil corrupted by thorns, and the good ground. The dirt of the wayside is an illustration of that which is outside the sower's field (the visible Church) and is therefore not relevant to our discussion, being an obvious reference to those who reject the Gospel outright and claim no fellowship whatsoever with Christ. The second and the third soils, however, are included within the boundaries of the field, though on its outer perimeters. These refer to those who outwardly associate themselves with the Church and, to at least some degree, receive some of its blessings, but inwardly retain an allegiance to and a desire for the sinful lifestyle they apparently aban-

---

covenant that I will make with the house of Israel after those days, says the LORD: I will put My law in their minds, and write it on their hearts; and I will be their God, and they shall be My people" (Jeremiah 31:33; cf. Ezekiel 36:25-27). They therefore "delight in the law of God according to the inward man" (Romans 7:22). The reprobate, however, who for whatever selfish reason associates himself with Christ, does need to be imposed upon by these conditions so that his hypocrisy may be manifest not only to others, but to himself as well.

doned so that they are eventually enticed back into the world. Only those of the fourth group, represented by the good ground, remain in the Church and grow to "bear fruits worthy of repentance" (Matthew 3:8). Christ said, "A good man out of the good treasure of his heart brings forth good; and an evil man out of the evil treasure of his heart brings forth evil. For out of the abundance of the heart his mouth speaks" (Luke 6:45). We cannot, therefore, entertain the thought that the second and third groups are in fact true believers, but instead they are examples of tares amidst the wheat (Mark 13:24). It is not a mere profession of faith in Christ that is evidence of true salvation, but a life that is increasingly "conformed to the image of [God's] Son, that He might be the firstborn among many brethren" (Romans 8:29).

Returning to the sixth chapter of Hebrews, we see exactly this distinction being made between the land which "bears herbs useful for those by whom it is cultivated," and the land that "bears thorns and briers." Since "a good tree cannot bear bad fruit, nor can a bad tree bear good fruit" (Matthew 7:18), these are those who outwardly align themselves with the Savior, but inwardly are not known by Him:

> "Not everyone who says to Me, 'Lord, Lord,' shall enter the kingdom of heaven, but he who does the will of My Father in heaven. Many will say to Me in that day, 'Lord, Lord, have we not prophesied in Your name, cast out demons in Your name, and done many wonders in Your name?' And then I will declare to them, 'I never knew you; depart from Me, you who practice lawlessness!'" (Matthew 7:21-23).

Judas Iscariot Was a False Professor

The writer of Hebrews continued on in verse 4 to speak of those who "were made partakers of the Holy Spirit." Reformed commentators have unanimously interpreted this phrase as a reference to the temporal bestowal of the miracle-working power and other external graces of the Holy Spirit upon the religious unregenerate who associate themselves with the Church. That the reprobate may temporarily possess spiritual gifts is evident throughout both the Old and New Testaments, the most notable of which was Judas Iscariot. There is no doubt that the supernatural gifts of healing, casting out of demons, etc., as well as the ability to herald the coming Kingdom, were equally present with Judas as with the other eleven disciples, for he was never suspected to be an enemy by those with whom he associated so closely for the three and a half years of Christ's earthly ministry.

Arminians, of course, would claim Judas as a prime example of a true believer who eventually apostatized, pointing out that he had intimate contact with Christ for an extended amount of time, he fellowshipped with other believers, and even exhibited the aforementioned gifts of the Holy Spirit.[19] All of these "evidences," however, were but external in nature. It is the heart of a man, though hidden to others around him, that is, as Hebrews 4:13 states, "naked and open to the eyes of Him to whom we must give account." The fact that Judas was able to delude his companions for so long is certainly not conclusive proof that he was truly regenerate. Indeed, Christ knew from the very beginning

---

19. Corner, *Believer's Security*, pages 32-34.

that Judas' "faith" was temporary and that he was motivated by greed and selfish ambition rather than by a genuine love for God. In fact, long before Judas visibly apostatized, Jesus had referred to him as "a devil" (John 6:70). The comments of Louis Berkhof are instructive:

> They are in the covenant . . . as far as the common covenant blessings are concerned. Though they do not experience the regenerating influence of the Holy Spirit, yet they are subject to certain special operations and influences of the Holy Spirit. The Spirit strives with them in a special manner, convicts them of sin, enlightens them in a measure, and enriches them with the blessings of common grace.[20]

It is clear that the myth of free will lies at the heart of the Arminian's misunderstanding of this passage in Hebrews. It is assumed that since men are supposedly able to choose to be saved, it must follow that if they have also chosen to join themselves to the visible Church then they are to be viewed as truly regenerate and never suspected to be otherwise. Keeping in mind the biblical doctrine of fallen man's inability to change his own spiritual condition, the Calvinist rejects this as a false assumption, pointing out such imposters as yet another example of man's depravity. Not all who followed Christ during His earthly ministry did so out of genuine love for Him and acceptance of what He taught. Multitudes were initially attracted to Him because of what benefits they might receive at His hands, such as free meals, healings, social prestige and recognition, or even the presumption of eternal life (Matthew 19:16). Today, the situation

---

20. Berkhof, *Systematic Theology*, page 289.

is no different. Thousands upon thousands are lured forward in "altar calls" to a god who promises health, wealth, emotional healing, and a boost to self-esteem, but when the bid to "come and die" is given, these hypocrites are nowhere to be found.

As pointed out by Matthew Henry, "among these who are nominal Christians, there are many who are real infidels."[21] Though believers may oftentimes be fooled by these "ravenous wolves" in "sheep's clothing" (Matthew 7:15), perceiving their apparent display of religious affection as evidence of true saving faith, "the unbelief of hypocrites is naked and open before the eyes of Christ."[22] As mentioned before, Christ will deny having ever known these professed Christians, and yet in John 10:14 we are told that He does, in fact, know His sheep. Unless one is willing to attribute a faulty memory to the omniscient Lord, we are forced to conclude that such apostates were never known by Christ because they were never His sheep.

Hebrews 6:4-8 and other similar passages stand as solemn warnings to such men as these to, as Paul stated, "Examine yourselves as to whether you are in the faith. Test yourselves" (2 Corinthians 13:5). However, the writer concluded his warning to the hypocrites by turning his attention to and offering the following words of comfort to the genuine believers in his audience: "But, beloved, we are confident of better things concerning you, yes, things that accompany salvation, though we speak in this manner" (Hebrews 6:9). An obvious distinction was made here by the writer of this

---

21. Henry, *Commentary*, page 1541.

22. Henry, *ibid*.

epistle between the things previously spoken of – the temporary faith and diseased fruit of those who fall away – and the "better things . . . that accompany salvation." These "better things" are described in the subsequent verses as persevering "work and labor of love" (verse 10), "diligence to the full assurance of hope until the end" (verse 11), and "faith and patience" which will "inherit the promises" (verse 12). Thus, rather than supporting the Arminian claim that true believers can "potentially go to hell,"[23] this passage instead offers conclusive testimony that, while leaving the reprobate to themselves, God will faithfully preserve those whom He has elected to salvation in Christ: "'Now the just shall live by faith; but if anyone draws back, My soul has no pleasure in him.' But we are not of those who draw back to perdition, but of those who believe to the saving of the soul" (Hebrews 10:38-39).

The Holy Spirit is the Guarantor of Salvation

As before, the importance of allowing Scripture to interpret itself must again be stressed. It may be granted that there are a handful of passages which can be interpreted in such a way as to deny the perseverance of the saints. However, the overwhelming message of the New Testament is that believers are securely held by the power and will of God. Thus, the difficult few should be interpreted in light of the easily-understood many, not vice versa. Below are given but a selection of a multitude of passages which offer assurance to the true believer:

---

23. Corner, *Believer's Security*, page 96.

There is therefore now no condemnation to those who are in Christ Jesus, who do not walk according to the flesh, but according to the Spirit. For the law of the Spirit of life in Christ Jesus has made me free from the law of sin and death. . . .

What then shall we say to these things? If God is for us, who can be against us? He who did not spare His own Son, but delivered Him up for us all, how shall He not with Him also freely give us all things? Who shall bring a charge against God's elect? It is God who justifies. Who is he who condemns? It is Christ who died, and furthermore is also risen, who is even at the right hand of God, who also makes intercession for us. . . .

For I am persuaded that neither death nor life, nor angels nor principalities nor powers, nor things present nor things to come, nor height nor depth, nor any other created thing, shall be able to separate us from the love of God which is in Christ Jesus our Lord (Romans 8:1-2, 31-34, 38-39).

Now He who establishes us with you in Christ and has anointed us is God, who also has sealed us and given us the Spirit in our hearts as a guarantee (2 Corinthians 1:21-22).

In Him you also trusted, after you heard the word of truth, the gospel of your salvation; in whom also, having believed, you were sealed with the Holy Spirit of promise, who is the guarantee of our inheritance until the redemption of the purchased possession, to the praise of His glory (Ephesians 1:13-14).

I thank my God upon every remembrance of you, always in every prayer of mine making request for you all with joy, for your fellowship in the gospel from the first day until now, being confident of this very thing, that He who has begun a good work in you will complete it until the day of Jesus Christ (Philippians 1:3-6).

Paul consistently taught that God's grace was bestowed upon His elect "not of works, lest anyone should boast" (Ephesians 2:9). How then could he elsewhere teach that, once saved and sealed by the Holy Spirit, a man's salvation is thereafter sustained, not by God's faithfulness to His promises, but rather by his own good works? Indeed, the entire epistle to the Galatians was written as a direct refutation of such a heresy as this. In Galatians 3:3, Paul asked, "Are you so foolish? Having begun in the Spirit, are you now being made perfect by the flesh?" It is true that he also exhorted the believer in Philippians 2:12 to "work out your own salvation with fear and trembling," but the very next verse should put this duty in its proper perspective: "[F]or it is God who works in you both to will and to do for His good pleasure." What is the "good pleasure" of God? Let the Lord Jesus Himself answer: "Do not fear, little flock, for it is your Father's good pleasure to give you the kingdom" (Luke 12:32). If it is God's "good pleasure" to give His elect eternal life, and He not only seals His people with the Holy Spirit but also works in their hearts to accomplish this end, can it be doubted that His purpose will be accomplished? Let such an impious thought return to the pit from whence it came.

Though the Christian is to be ever mindful of maintaining a holy life, he is nevertheless not to fear the loss of his eternal inheritance in heaven should he ever stumble in his walk with Christ.[24] Just as an earthly father holds his own

---

24. This is certainly not to lend credence to the antinomian "easy be-

lievism" that is so prevalent in modern Evangelicalism. In his book, *The Gospel According to Jesus*, John MacArthur demolished the false idea that Christ can be accepted as one's Savior but not necessarily as one's Lord, and that someone can thereafter live like a devil and still be considered a saint whose salvation is "eternally secure" ([Grand Rapids, Michigan: Zondervan Publishing Company, 2008). That this is really what is being taught by the proponents of "eternal security" is easily demonstrated from their own writings. According to R. B. Thieme, a professing Christian can even go so far as to completely turn his back on God and still be a "Christian atheist," and therefore eternally secure: "It is possible, even probable, that when a believer out of fellowship falls for certain types of philosophy, if he is a logical thinker, he will become an 'unbelieving believer.' Yet believers who become agnostics are still saved; they are still born again. You can even become an atheist; but if you once accept Christ as saviour, you cannot lose your salvation, even though you deny God" (*Apes and Peacocks: The Pursuit of Happiness* [Houston, Texas: self-published, 1973], page 23). This same basic idea is also taught by popular Southern Baptist pastor Charles Stanley in his book entitled, *Eternal Security*: "The Bible clearly teaches that God's love for His people is of such magnitude that even those who walk away from the faith have not the slightest chance of slipping from His hand. . . . Even if a believer for all practical purposes becomes an unbeliever, his salvation is not in jeopardy . . . . [B]elievers who lose or abandon their faith will retain their salvation. . . ." (pages 74, 93, 94)

The Calvinist doctrine of assurance, of course, bears no resemblance whatsoever to this ridiculous assertion. Since the Bible teaches that no man can "accept Jesus" in the first place without first having been regenerated by the Holy Spirit, the Christ who is embraced by the true believer will be the whole Christ, not the divided christ of the modern Arminian pulpit. Arthur W. Pink rightly noted, "There is a deadly and damnable heresy being widely propagated today to the effect that, if a sinner truly accepts Christ as his personal Saviour, no matter how he lives afterwards, he cannot perish. That is a satanic lie. . . ." (quoted by Iain H. Murray, *The Life of A. W. Pink* [Edinburgh, Scotland: The Banner of Truth Trust, 1981], page 248).

This is not to claim, however, that sin is so entirely eradicated from child securely by the hand, the heavenly Father so holds those who have trusted in Him to save them. Furthermore, the Holy Spirit has taken up residence within his heart as Comforter and Chastener – the first in times of distress; the latter in times of sin. It is this same Spirit who will never leave the redeemed child of God, for "the gifts and the calling of God are irrevocable" (Romans 11:29).

Christ's Promise of Eternal Life

If the testimony of the Apostle Paul is not sufficient to convince the obstinate Arminian, we turn now to the words of our Savior Himself. In Luke 22:32, Jesus prayed for Peter that his faith would not fail. That this prayer was not for Peter's sake only, but for all Christians, is clearly seen in Christ's final prayer at the Passover meal:

> "I pray for them. I do not pray for the world but for those whom You have given Me, for they are Yours. And all Mine are Yours, and Yours are Mine, and I am glorified in them. Now I am no longer in the world, but these are in the world, and I come to You. Holy Father, keep through Your name those whom You have given Me, that they may be one as We are. While I was with them in the world, I kept them in Your name. Those whom You gave Me I have kept; and none of them is lost except the son of perdition,

---

the Christian's life that he will always act consistently with his election and calling, but that the overruling motive of his heart is a Spirit-led desire to obey Christ. This was the meaning of Christ's words in Matthew 7:16: "You will know them by their fruits." To denounce this teaching as a legalistic addition of works to faith in order to procure salvation, as Zane Hodges did in his best-selling response to MacArthur entitled, *The Gospel Under Seige*, is deplorable ignorance of the biblical Gospel.

that the Scripture might be fulfilled. . . .

"I do not pray that You should take them out of the world, but that You should keep them from the evil one. . . . Father, I desire that they also whom You gave Me may be with Me where I am, that they may behold My glory which You have given Me; for You loved Me before the foundation of the world" (John 17:9-12, 15, 24).

In John 11:42, we read of Christ's confidence that His prayers were always heard by the Father. In light of His promise in John 14:16 ("And I will pray the Father, and He will give . . . ."), it would be impious to insinuate that Christ's Passover prayer was not heard by the Father, and that some of God's elect could indeed perish. How dare any man, especially a professed believer, belie the very words of the Son of God when He said, "All that the Father gives Me will come to Me, and the one who comes to Me I will by no means cast out. For I have come down from heaven, not to do My own will, but the will of Him who sent Me. This is the will of the Father who sent Me, that of all He has given Me I should lose nothing, but should raise it up at the last day" (John 6:37-39). Surely it cannot be claimed that Christ is somehow lacking in His ability to fulfill the Father's will that He keep those who have been entrusted to His care, or that He will ever violate His holy trust by driving one of the elect away.[25] No, the Arminian may answer, Christ would not reject the believer unless he first rejects Christ.[26] How-

---

25. The original Greek of verse 37 reads, οὐ μὴ ἐκβάλω ἔξω (*ou mé ekbálō exō*). Being a double negative, this phrase can be literally translated as, "No, not at all will I cast him out."

26. According to Daniel Corner, "[Christ's] powerful prayers and our free will work together. Our free will can, however, override His in-

ever, this reply ignores the fact that the love instilled in the hearts of God's elect is not the fickle affection produced by a man-centered "gospel." To the contrary, the love which the true believer has toward God keeps His commandments (John 14:15), believes and endures (1 Corinthians 13:7), and never fails (1 Corinthians 13:8). The elect cannot and will not reject Christ because they are "members of His body, of His flesh and of His bones" (Ephesians 5:30; cf. 1 Corinthians 6:17).

Against the attacks of Arminianism, God's promise to those who really belong to Him stands firm and true:

> They shall be My people, and I will be their God; then I will give them one heart and one way, that they may fear Me forever, for the good of them and their children after them. And I will make an everlasting covenant with them, that I will not turn away from doing them good; but I will put My fear in their hearts so that they will not depart from Me (Jeremiah 32:38-40).

> "For God so loved the world that He gave His only begotten Son, that whoever believes in Him should not perish but have everlasting life. . . .
> "My sheep hear My voice, and I know them, and they follow Me. And I give them eternal life, and they shall never perish; neither shall anyone snatch them out of My hand. My Father, who has given them to Me, is greater than all; and no one is able to snatch them out of My Father's hand. I and My Father are one" (John 3:16, 10:27-30).

---

credibly powerful prayers and His will for us" (*Believer's Security*, page 69). Corner thus makes God the servant of the human will, rather than vice versa, as the Bible teaches (Proverbs 21:1; Philippians 2:13). This is sheer atheism.

Do Arminians Slander the Godhead?

In his essay for *The Grace of God/The Will of Man*, William Abraham wrote, "It is Calvinists, not Arminians, who have a problem in providing adequate resources for a healthy doctrine of assurance. It is small wonder then that those who have meditated thoroughly on the doctrines of Calvinism in a personal and existential way have been driven at times to despair."[27] In light of what we have seen of the doctrines of Calvinism, the absurdity of such a remark goes without saying. After all, what greater basis can there possibly be for a "healthy assurance" than the faithfulness of the eternal, immutable, and sovereign God? Can it be said that a God who is omnipotent in drawing sinners to Himself is lacking in power to keep saints from falling away? If, while we were "enmity against God" (Romans 8:7), and "children of wrath" (Ephesians 2:3), and "enemies in [our] minds by wicked works" (Colossians 1:21), the Father demonstrated His mercy and love by redeeming us through His Son, why then would He disown us now that we are "accepted in the Beloved" (Ephesians 1:6)? Can the true Christian, whose very nature has been changed by the indwelling Spirit, ever find himself in a condition that surpasses his former state of rebellion and wickedness? One could hardly think so: "If God justified and reconciled us when we were enemies, much more will he save us when we are justified and reconciled. He that has done the greater, which is of enemies to make us friends, will certainly do the less, which is when we are friends, to use us friendly and to be kind to us."[28]

---

27. Abraham, "Predestination and Assurance," page 235.

28. Henry, *Commentary*, page 1765.

The doctrine that a saint can fall from grace, while attempting to uphold the believer's responsibility to live a holy life, actually slanders the very Godhead itself. First of all, it denigrates the omniscience of the Father, who, in electing individuals for eternal life, failed to take into account those postregenerational sins which would later disqualify them for heaven. Secondly, it demeans the atoning sacrifice of the Son by implying that in shedding His blood, Christ did not provide a full propitiation for sin, but only a partial payment to which the believer must himself continue to enhance by his own faithfulness. And finally, it blasphemes the Holy Spirit by declaring that He who is powerful enough to regenerate a lost sinner is somehow unable to maintain and preserve His own work. Though such a teaching is compatible with the finite godism of Clark Pinnock's process theology,[29] a deity that is not all knowing, a savior that does not fully save, and a preserver that is impotent to keep his own, bear no resemblance to the Persons of the Almighty Trinity revealed in Scripture. The false godhead of Arminianism is therefore an idol.

To be sure, nearly all Christians have known someone who maintained a religious facade for a time, perhaps even for years, and yet eventually turned his back on Christ, never to return. We all can bring to mind at least one individual who was once doctrinally sound and active in sharing the Gospel with others, and yet now is found entangled in a false belief system which denies the essential tenets of the biblical faith. The task before us is not to determine how to interpret the Bible to fit our experiences, but how to interpret and conform our experiences according to the clear teachings

---

30. See Appendix Three.

of Scripture. When faced with a troubling instance of apostasy, we need look no further than 1 John 2:19 for the reason: "They went out from us, but they were not of us; for if they had been of us, they would have continued with us; but they went out that they might be made manifest, that none of them were of us."

CONCLUSION

"Arminianism, because it obscures the glory which belongs solely to the grace of God, comes under the apostolic condemnation and is therefore an error sufficiently serious for there to be no room for compromising."[1] By now the reader should be convinced that the popular soteriological system known as "Arminianism" is not biblical and is not Christian. Though using much of the same terminology as orthodox Christianity, Arminianism actually corrupts the message of the Scriptures to such an extent that "a different gospel" (Galatians 1:6) emerges which bears only an outward resemblance to the genuine Gospel. So serious are the aberrations of this false gospel that no one can be saved who really understands it and believes it.

In 2 Corinthians 11:4, the Apostle Paul wrote, "For if he who comes preaches another Jesus whom we have not preached, or if you receive a different spirit which you have not received, or a different gospel which you have not accepted – you may well put up with it!" Surely Paul, who surrendered his own life to "preach Christ crucified" (1 Corinthians 1:23), would be greatly distressed to see the con-

---

1. Murray, *Forgotten Spurgeon*, page 81.

dition of the professing Church today. Amidst the syrupy cesspool of self-exalting preaching, and the meaningless prattle of "Jesus loves you and has a wonderful plan for your life," what is really needed is a voice in the wilderness of modern Evangelicalism asking the question, "Which Jesus?" It is not enough to merely hang a painting of Jesus in one's home, or to speak of Him to others with quivering emotion in one's voice. It is not enough to merely display a cross on the wall of the church building upon which the congregation may gaze with warm feelings or "goose bumps." If the Jesus we proclaim, and the cross which we adore are not biblical, then our "gospel" is nothing but the cultish pulpiteering of a lie which will damn both ourselves and our hearers.

Indeed, no more fitting label may be applied to the entire Arminian system than that of a damning lie. As "a bad tree cannot bear good fruit" (Matthew 7:18), many of the ethical problems which plague modern Evangelicalism can be traced right back to the man-centered theology of Arminianism, which reduces God to a sappy, enfeebled geriatric who is ever fearful of "coming on too strong." It is no wonder that such a god fails to stir up a deep reverence and worship within the hearts of his devotees:

> The new gospel [of Arminianism] conspicuously fails to produce deep reverence, deep repentance, deep humility, a spirit of worship, a concern for the church. Why? We would suggest that the reason lies in its own character and content. It fails to make men God-centered in their hearts. . . . One way of stating the difference between it and the old gospel is to say that it is too exclusively concerned to be "helpful" to man – to bring peace, comfort, happiness, satisfaction – and too little concerned to glorify God. The

old gospel['s] . . . first concern was always to give glory to God.[2]

Whether we are dealing with the subject of predestination, the Atonement, God's effectual drawing of His elect to Himself, or His preservation of the same, the sovereign freedom of the Almighty to do with His creatures as He pleases must be affirmed in every area of our theology lest, as John Owen warned, we "arm the clay against the potter."[3] The following passages of Scripture will suffice to conclude our examination of Arminianism:

> "O LORD God of our fathers, are You not God in heaven, and do You not rule over all the kingdoms of the nations, and in Your hand is there not power and might, so that no one is able to withstand You?" (2 Chronicles 20:6)

> All the inhabitants of the earth are reputed as nothing; He does according to His will in the army of heaven and among the inhabitants of the earth. No one can restrain His hand or say to Him, "What have You done?" (Daniel 4:35)

---

2. Packer, "Introductory Essay," pages 1-2.
3. Owen, "Display of Arminianism," page 20.

APPENDIX ONE
The Canons of Dordt

The First Head of Doctrine:
Divine Election and Reprobation

Article 1: *God's Right to Condemn All People.* Since all people have sinned in Adam and have come under the sentence of the curse and eternal death, God would have done no one an injustice if it had been his will to leave the entire human race in sin and under the curse, and to condemn them on account of their sin. As the apostle says: "The whole world is liable to the condemnation of God" (Rom. 3:19), "All have sinned and are deprived of the glory of God" (Rom. 3:23), and "The wages of sin is death" (Rom. 6:23).

Article 2: *The Manifestation of God's Love.* But this is how God showed his love: he sent his only begotten Son into the world, so that whoever believes in him should not perish but have eternal life.

Article 3: *The Preaching of the Gospel.* In order that people may be brought to faith, God mercifully sends proclaimers of this very joyful message to the people he wishes and at the time he wishes. By this ministry people are called to repentance and faith in Christ crucified. "For how shall they believe in him of whom they have not heard? And how shall they hear without someone preaching? And how shall they preach unless they have been sent?" (Rom. 10:14-15).

Article 4: *A Twofold Response to the Gospel*. God's anger remains on those who do not believe this gospel. But those who do accept it and embrace Jesus the Savior with a true and living faith are delivered through him from God's anger and from destruction, and receive the gift of eternal life.

Article 5: *The Sources of Unbelief and of Faith*. The cause or blame for this unbelief, as well as for all other sins, is not at all in God, but in man. Faith in Jesus Christ, however, and salvation through him is a free gift of God. As Scripture says, "It is by grace you have been saved, through faith, and this not from yourselves; it is a gift of God" (Eph. 2:8). Likewise: "It has been freely given to you to believe in Christ" (Phil. 1:29).

Article 6: *God's Eternal Decision*. The fact that some receive from God the gift of faith within time, and that others do not, stems from his eternal decision. "For all his works are known to God from eternity" (Acts 15:18; Eph. 1:11). In accordance with this decision he graciously softens the hearts, however hard, of his chosen ones and inclines them to believe, but by his just judgment he leaves in their wickedness and hardness of heart those who have not been chosen. And in this especially is disclosed to us his act – unfathomable, and as merciful as it is just – of distinguishing between people equally lost. This is the well-known decision of election and reprobation revealed in God's Word. This decision the wicked, impure, and unstable distort to their own ruin, but it provides holy and godly souls with comfort beyond words.

Article 7: *Election*. Election is God's unchangeable purpose by which he did the following:

Before the foundation of the world, by sheer grace, according to the free good pleasure of his will, he chose in Christ to salvation a definite number of particular people out of the entire human race, which had fallen by its own fault from its original innocence into sin and ruin. Those chosen were neither better nor more deserving than the others, but lay with them in the common misery. He did this in Christ, whom he also appointed from eternity to be the mediator, the head of all those chosen, and the foundation of their salvation. And so he decided to give the chosen ones to Christ to be saved, and to call and draw them effectively into Christ's fellowship through his Word and Spirit. In other words, he decided to grant them true faith in Christ, to justify them, to sanctify them, and finally, after powerfully preserving them in the fellowship of his Son, to glorify them.

God did all this in order to demonstrate his mercy, to the praise of the riches of his glorious grace. As Scripture says, "God chose us in Christ, before the foundation of the world, so that we should be holy and blameless before him with love; he predestined us whom he adopted as his children through Jesus Christ, in himself, according to the good pleasure of his will, to the praise of his glorious grace, by which he freely made us pleasing to himself in his beloved" (Eph. 1:4-6). And elsewhere, "Those whom he predestined, he also called; and those whom he called, he also justified; and those whom he justified, he also glorified" (Rom. 8:30).

Article 8: *A Single Decision of Election*. This election is not of many kinds; it is one and the same election for all who were to be saved in the Old and the New Testament. For Scripture declares that there is a single good pleasure, purpose, and plan of God's will, by which he chose us from eternity both to grace and to glory, both to salvation and to the way of salvation, which he prepared in advance for us to walk in.

Article 9: *Election Not Based on Foreseen Faith*. This same election took place, not on the basis of foreseen faith, of the obedience of faith, of holiness, or of any other good quality and disposition, as though it were based on a prerequisite cause or condition in the person to be chosen, but rather for the purpose of faith, of the obedience of faith, of holiness, and so on. Accordingly, election is the source of each of the benefits of salvation. Faith, holiness, and the other saving gifts, and at last eternal life itself, flow forth from election as its fruits and effects. As the apostle says, "He chose us [not because we were, but] so that we should be holy and blameless before him in love" (Eph. 1:4).

Article 10: *Election Based on God's Good Pleasure*. But the cause of this undeserved election is exclusively the good pleasure of God. This does not involve his choosing certain human qualities or actions from among all those possible as a condition of salvation, but rather involves his adopting certain particular persons from among the common mass of sinners as his own possession. As Scripture says, "When the children were not yet born, and had done nothing either good or bad . . . , she [Rebecca] was told, 'The older will serve the younger.' As it is written, 'Jacob I loved, but Esau I hated'" (Rom. 9:11-13). Also, "All who were appointed for eternal life believed" (Acts 13:48).

Article 11: *Election Unchangeable*. Just as God himself is

most wise, unchangeable, all-knowing, and almighty, so the election made by him can neither be suspended nor altered, revoked, or annulled; neither can his chosen ones be cast off, nor their number reduced.

Article 12: *The Assurance of Election*. Assurance of this their eternal and unchangeable election to salvation is given to the chosen in due time, though by various stages and in differing measure. Such assurance comes not by inquisitive searching into the hidden and deep things of God, but by noticing within themselves, with spiritual joy and holy delight, the unmistakable fruits of election pointed out in God's Word – such as a true faith in Christ, a childlike fear of God, a godly sorrow for their sins, a hunger and thirst for righteousness, and so on.

Article 13: *The Fruit of This Assurance*. In their awareness and assurance of this election God's children daily find greater cause to humble themselves before God, to adore the fathomless depth of his mercies, to cleanse themselves, and to give fervent love in return to him who first so greatly loved them. This is far from saying that this teaching concerning election, and reflection upon it, make God's children lax in observing his commandments or carnally self-assured. By God's just judgment this does usually happen to those who casually take for granted the grace of election or engage in idle and brazen talk about it but are unwilling to walk in the ways of the chosen.

Article 14: *Teaching Election Properly*. Just as, by God's wise plan, this teaching concerning divine election has been proclaimed through the prophets, Christ himself, and the apostles, in Old and New Testament times, and has subsequently been committed to writing in the Holy Scriptures, so also today in God's church, for which it was specifically intended, this teaching must be set forth – with a spirit of discretion, in a godly and holy manner, at the appropriate time and place, without inquisitive searching into the ways of the Most High. This must be done for the glory of God's most holy name, and for the lively comfort of his people.

Article 15: *Reprobation.* Moreover, Holy Scripture most especially highlights this eternal and undeserved grace of our election and brings it out more clearly for us, in that it further bears witness that not all people have been chosen but that some have not been chosen or have been passed by in God's eternal election – those, that is, concerning whom God, on the basis of his entirely free, most just, irreproachable, and unchangeable good pleasure, made the following decision: to leave them in the common misery into which, by their own fault, they have plunged themselves; not to grant them saving faith and the grace of conversion; but finally to condemn and eternally punish them (having been left in their own ways and under his just judgment), not only for their unbelief but also for all their other sins, in order to display his justice. And this is the decision of reprobation, which does not at all make God the author of sin (a blasphemous thought!) but rather its fearful, irreproachable, just judge and avenger.

Article 16: *Responses to the Teaching of Reprobation.* Those who do not yet actively experience within themselves a living faith in Christ or an assured confidence of heart, peace of conscience, a zeal for childlike obedience, and a glorying in God through Christ, but who nevertheless use the means by which God has promised to work these things in us – such people ought not to be alarmed at the mention of reprobation, nor to count themselves among the reprobate; rather they ought to continue diligently in the use of the means, to desire fervently a time of more abundant grace, and to wait for it in reverence and humility. On the other hand, those who seriously desire to turn to God, to be pleasing to him alone, and to be delivered from the body of death, but are not yet able to make such progress along the way of godliness and faith as they would like – such people ought much less to stand in fear of the teaching concerning reprobation, since our merciful God has promised that he will not snuff out a smoldering wick and that he will not break a bruised reed. However, those who have forgotten God and their Savior Jesus Christ and have abandoned themselves wholly to the cares of the world and the pleasures of the flesh – such people have every reason to stand in fear of this teaching, as long as they do not seriously turn to God.

Article 17: *The Salvation of the Infants of Believers*. Since we must make judgments about God's will from his Word, which testifies that the children of believers are holy, not by nature but by virtue of the gracious covenant in which they together with their parents are included, godly parents ought not to doubt the election and salvation of their children whom God calls out of this life in infancy.

Article 18: *The Proper Attitude Toward Election and Reprobation*. To those who complain about this grace of an undeserved election and about the severity of a just reprobation, we reply with the words of the apostle, "Who are you, O man, to talk back to God?" (Rom. 9:20), and with the words of our Savior, "Have I no right to do what I want with my own?" (Matt. 20:15). We, however, with reverent adoration of these secret things, cry out with the apostle: "Oh, the depths of the riches both of the wisdom and the knowledge of God! How unsearchable are his judgments, and his ways beyond tracing out! For who has known the mind of the Lord? Or who has been his counselor? Or who has first given to God, that God should repay him? For from him and through him and to him are all things. To him be the glory forever! Amen" (Rom. 11:33-36).

Rejection of Errors

Having set forth the orthodox teaching concerning election and reprobation, the Synod rejects the errors of those –

First. Who teach that the will of God to save those who would believe and persevere in faith and in the obedience of faith is the whole and entire decision of election to salvation, and that nothing else concerning this decision has been revealed in God's Word.

For they deceive the simple and plainly contradict Holy Scripture in its testimony that God does not only wish to save those who would believe, but that he has also from eternity chosen certain particular people to whom, rather than to others, he would within time grant faith in Christ and perseverance. As Scripture says, "I have revealed your name to those whom you gave me" (John 17:6). Likewise, "All who were appointed for eternal life believed" (Acts 13:48), and "He chose us before the foundation of the world so that we should be holy. . . ." (Eph. 1:4)

Second. Who teach that God's election to eternal life is of many kinds: one general and indefinite, the other particular and definite; and the latter in turn either incomplete, revocable, nonperemptory, or else complete, irrevocable, and peremptory. Likewise, who teach that there is one election to faith and another to salvation, so that there can be an election to justifying faith apart from a peremptory election to salvation.

For this is an invention of the human brain, devised apart from the Scriptures, which distorts the teaching concerning election and breaks up this golden chain of salvation: "Those whom he predestined, he also called; and those whom he called, he also justified; and those whom he justified, he also glorified" (Rom. 8:30).

Third. Who teach that God's good pleasure and purpose, which Scripture mentions in its teaching of election, does not involve God's choosing certain particular people rather than others, but involves God's choosing, out of all possible conditions (including the works of the law) or out of the whole order of things, the intrinsically unworthy act of faith, as well as the imperfect obedience of faith, to be a condition of salvation; and it involves his graciously wishing to count this as perfect obedience and to look upon it as worthy of the reward of eternal life.

For by this pernicious error the good pleasure of God and the merit of Christ are robbed of their effectiveness and people are drawn away, by unprofitable inquiries, from the truth of undeserved justification and from the simplicity of the Scriptures. It also gives the lie to these words of the apostle: "God called us with a holy calling, not in virtue of works, but in virtue of his own purpose and the grace which was given to us in Christ Jesus before the beginning of time" (2 Tim. 1:9).

Fourth. Who teach that in election to faith a prerequisite condition is that man should rightly use the light of nature, be upright, unassuming, humble, and disposed to eternal life, as though election depended to some extent on these factors.

For this smacks of Pelagius, and it clearly calls into question the words of the apostle: "We lived at one time in the passions of our flesh, following the will of our flesh and thoughts, and we were by nature children of wrath, like everyone else. But God, who is rich in mercy, out of the great love with which he loved us, even when we were dead in transgressions, made us alive with Christ, by whose grace you have been saved. And God raised us up with him and seated us with him in heaven in Christ Jesus, in order that in the coming ages we might show the surpassing riches of his grace, according to his kindness toward us in Christ Jesus. For it is by grace you have been saved, through faith (and this not from yourselves; it is the gift of God) not by works, so that no one can boast" (Eph. 2:3-9).

Fifth. Who teach that the incomplete and nonperemptory election of particular persons to salvation occurred on the basis of a foreseen faith, repentance, holiness, and godliness, which has just begun or continued for some time; but that complete and peremptory election occurred on the basis of a foreseen perseverance to the end in faith, repentance, holiness, and godliness. And that this is the gracious and evangelical worthiness, on account of which the one who is chosen is more worthy than the one who is not chosen. And therefore that faith, the obedience of faith, holiness, godliness, and perseverance are not fruits or effects of an unchangeable election to glory, but indispensable conditions and causes, which are prerequisite in those who are to be chosen in the complete election, and which are foreseen as achieved in them.

This runs counter to the entire Scripture, which throughout impresses upon our ears and hearts these sayings among others: "Election is not by works, but by him who calls" (Rom. 9:11-12); "All who were appointed for eternal life believed" (Acts 13:48); "He chose us in himself so that we should be holy" (Eph. 1:4); "You did not choose me, but I chose you" (John 15:16); "If by grace, not by works" (Rom. 11:6); "In this is love, not that we loved God, but that he loved us and sent his Son" (1 John 4:10).

Sixth. Who teach that not every election to salvation is unchangeable, but that some of the chosen can perish and do in fact perish eternally, with no decision of God to prevent it.

By this gross error they make God changeable, destroy the comfort of the godly concerning the steadfastness of their election, and contradict the Holy Scriptures, which teach that the elect cannot be led astray (Matt. 24:24), that Christ does not lose those given to him by the Father (John 6:39), and that those whom God predestined, called, and justified, he also glorifies (Rom. 8:30).

Seventh. Who teach that in this life there is no fruit, no awareness, and no assurance of one's unchangeable election to glory, except as conditional upon something changeable and contingent.

For not only is it absurd to speak of an uncertain assurance, but these things also militate against the experience of the saints, who with the apostle rejoice from an awareness of their election and sing the praises of this gift of God; who, as Christ urged, rejoice with his disciples that their names have been written in heaven (Luke 10:20); and finally who hold up against the flaming arrows of the devil's temptations the awareness of their election, with the question "Who will bring any charge against those whom God has chosen?" (Rom. 8:33).

Eighth. Who teach that it was not on the basis of his just will alone that God decided to leave anyone in the fall of Adam and in the common state of sin and condemnation or to pass anyone by in the imparting of grace necessary for faith and conversion.

For these words stand fast: "He has mercy on whom he wishes, and he hardens whom he wishes" (Rom. 9:18). And also: "To you it has been given to know the secrets of the kingdom of heaven, but to them it has not been given" (Matt. 13:11). Likewise: "I give glory to you, Father, Lord of heaven and earth, that you have hidden these things from the wise and understanding, and have revealed them to little children; yes, Father, because that was your pleasure" (Matt. 11:25-26).

Ninth. Who teach that the cause for God's sending the gospel to one people rather than to another is not merely and solely God's good pleasure, but rather that one people is better and worthier than the other to whom the gospel is not communicated.

For Moses contradicts this when he addresses the people of Israel as follows: "Behold, to Jehovah your God belong the heavens and the highest heavens, the earth and whatever is in it. But Jehovah was inclined in his affection to love your ancestors alone, and chose out their descendants after them, you above all peoples, as at this day" (Deut. 10:14-15). And also Christ: "Woe to you, Korazin! Woe to you, Bethsaida!

for if those mighty works done in you had been done in Tyre and Sidon, they would have repented long ago in sackcloth and ashes" (Matt. 11:21).

Second Head of Doctrine:
Christ's Death and Human Redemption

Article 1: *The Punishment Which God's Justice Requires.* God is not only supremely merciful, but also supremely just. His justice requires (as he has revealed himself in the Word) that the sins we have committed against his infinite majesty be punished with both temporal and eternal punishments, of soul as well as body. We cannot escape these punishments unless satisfaction is given to God's justice.

Article 2: *The Satisfaction Made by Christ.* Since, however, we ourselves cannot give this satisfaction or deliver ourselves from God's anger, God in his boundless mercy has given us as a guarantee his only begotten Son, who was made to be sin and a curse for us, in our place, on the cross, in order that he might give satisfaction for us.

Article 3: *The Infinite Value of Christ's Death.* This death of God's Son is the only and entirely complete sacrifice and satisfaction for sins; it is of infinite value and worth, more than sufficient to atone for the sins of the whole world.

Article 4: *Reasons for This Infinite Value.* This death is of such great value and worth for the reason that the person who suffered it is – as was necessary to be our Savior – not only a true and perfectly holy man, but also the only begotten Son of God, of the same eternal and infinite essence with the Father and the Holy Spirit. Another reason is that this death was accompanied by the experience of God's anger and curse, which we by our sins had fully deserved.

Article 5: *The Mandate to Proclaim the Gospel to All.* Moreover, it is the promise of the gospel that whoever believes in Christ crucified shall not perish but have eternal life. This promise, together with the command to repent and believe, ought to be announced and declared without differentiation or discrimination to all nations and people, to whom God in his good pleasure sends the gospel.

Article 6: *Unbelief Man's Responsibility.* However, that many who have been called through the gospel do not repent or believe in Christ but perish in unbelief is not because the sacrifice of Christ offered on the cross is deficient or insufficient, but because they themselves are at fault.

Article 7: *Faith God's Gift.* But all who genuinely believe and are delivered and saved by Christ's death from their sins and from destruction receive this favor solely from God's grace – which he owes to no one – given to them in Christ from eternity.

Article 8: *The Saving Effectiveness of Christ's Death.* For it was the entirely free plan and very gracious will and intention of God the Father that the enlivening and saving effectiveness of his Son's costly death should work itself out in all his chosen ones, in order that he might grant justifying faith to them only and thereby lead them without fail to salvation. In other words, it was God's will that Christ through the blood of the cross (by which he confirmed the new covenant) should effectively redeem from every people, tribe, nation, and language all those and only those who were chosen from eternity to salvation and given to him by the Father; that he should grant them faith (which, like the Holy Spirit's other saving gifts, he acquired for them by his death); that he should cleanse them by his blood from all their sins, both original and actual, whether committed before or after their coming to faith; that he should faithfully preserve them to the very end; and that he should finally present them to himself, a glorious people, without spot or wrinkle.

Article 9: *The Fulfillment of God's Plan.* This plan, arising out of God's eternal love for his chosen ones, from the beginning of the world to the present time has been powerfully carried out and will also be carried out in the future, the gates of hell seeking vainly to prevail against it. As a result the chosen are gathered into one, all in their own time, and there is always a church of believers founded on Christ's blood, a church which steadfastly loves, persistently worships, and – here and in all eternity – praises him as her Savior who laid down his life for her on the cross, as a bridegroom for his bride.

Rejection of Errors

Having set forth the orthodox teaching, the Synod rejects the errors of those –

First. Who teach that God the Father appointed his Son to death on the cross without a fixed and definite plan to save anyone by name, so that the necessity, usefulness, and worth of what Christ's death obtained could have stood intact and altogether perfect, complete and whole, even if the redemption that was obtained had never in actual fact been applied to any individual.

For this assertion is an insult to the wisdom of God the Father and to the merit of Jesus Christ, and it is contrary to Scripture. For the Savior speaks as follows: "I lay down my life for the sheep," and "I know them" (John 10:15, 27). And Isaiah the prophet says concerning the Savior: "When he shall make himself an offering for sin, he shall see his offspring, he shall prolong his days, and the will of Jehovah shall prosper in his hand" (Isa. 53:10). Finally, this undermines the article of the creed in which we confess what we believe concerning the Church.

Second. Who teach that the purpose of Christ's death was not to establish in actual fact a new covenant of grace by his blood, but only to acquire for the Father the mere right to enter once more into a covenant with men, whether of grace or of works.

For this conflicts with Scripture, which teaches that Christ has become the guarantee and mediator of a better – that is, a new – covenant (Heb. 7:22; 9:15), and that a will is in force only when someone has died (Heb. 9:17).

Third. Who teach that Christ, by the satisfaction which he gave, did not certainly merit for anyone salvation itself and the faith by which this satisfaction of Christ is effectively applied to salvation, but only acquired for the Father the authority or plenary will to relate in a new way with men and to impose such new conditions as he chose, and that the satisfying of these conditions depends on the free choice of man; consequently, that it was possible that either all or none would fulfill them.

For they have too low an opinion of the death of Christ, do not at all acknowledge the foremost fruit or benefit which it brings forth, and summon back from hell the Pelagian error.

Fourth. Who teach that what is involved in the new covenant of grace which God the Father made with men through the intervening of Christ's death is not that we are justified before God and saved through faith, insofar as it accepts Christ's merit, but rather that God, having withdrawn his demand for perfect obedience to the law, counts faith itself, and the imperfect obedience of faith, as perfect obedience to the law, and graciously looks upon this as worthy of the reward of eternal life.

For they contradict Scripture: "They are justified freely by his grace through the redemption that came by Jesus Christ, whom God presented as a sacrifice of atonement, through faith in his blood" (Rom. 3:24-25). And along with the ungodly Socinus, they introduce a new and foreign justification of man before God, against the consensus of the whole church.

Fifth. Who teach that all people have been received into the state of reconciliation and into the grace of the covenant, so that no one on account of original sin is liable to condemnation, or is to be condemned, but that all are free from the guilt of this sin. For this opinion conflicts with Scripture which asserts that we are by nature children of wrath.

Sixth. Who make use of the distinction between obtaining and applying in order to instill in the unwary and inexperienced the opinion that God, as far as he is concerned, wished to bestow equally upon all people the benefits which are gained by Christ's death; but that the distinction by which some rather than others come to share in the forgiveness of sins and eternal life depends on their own free choice (which applies itself to the grace offered indiscriminately) but does not depend on the unique gift of mercy which effectively works in them, so that they, rather than others, apply that grace to themselves.

For, while pretending to set forth this distinction in an acceptable sense, they attempt to give the people the deadly poison of Pelagianism.

Seventh. Who teach that Christ neither could die, nor had to die, nor did die for those whom God so dearly loved and chose to eternal life, since such people do not need the death of Christ.

For they contradict the apostle, who says: "Christ loved me and gave himself up for me" (Gal. 2:20), and likewise: "Who will bring any charge against those whom God has chosen? It is God who justifies. Who is he that condemns? It is Christ who died, that is, for them" (Rom. 8:33-34). They also contradict the Savior, who asserts: "I lay down my life for the sheep" (John 10:15), and "My command is this: Love one another as I have loved you. Greater love has no one than this, that one lay down his life for his friends" (John 15:12-13).

Third and Fourth Heads of Doctrine: Human Corruption and Conversion to God

Article 1: *The Effect of the Fall on Human Nature.* Man was originally created in the image of God and was furnished in his mind with a true and salutary knowledge of his Creator and things spiritual, in his will and heart with righteousness, and in all his emotions with purity; indeed, the whole man was holy. However, rebelling against God at the devil's instigation and by his own free will, he deprived himself of these outstanding gifts. Rather, in their place he brought upon himself blindness, terrible darkness, futility, and distortion of judgment in his mind; perversity, defiance, and hardness in his heart and will; and finally impurity in all his emotions.

Article 2: *The Spread of Corruption*. Man brought forth children of the same nature as himself after the fall. That is to say, being corrupt he brought forth corrupt children. The corruption spread, by God's just judgment, from Adam to all his descendants – except for Christ alone – not by way of imitation (as in former times the Pelagians would have it) but by way of the propagation of his perverted nature.

Article 3: *Total Inability*. Therefore, all people are conceived in sin and are born children of wrath, unfit for any saving good, inclined to evil, dead in their sins, and slaves to sin; without the grace of the regenerating Holy Spirit they are neither willing nor able to return to God, to reform their distorted nature, or even to dispose themselves to such reform.

Article 4: *The Inadequacy of the Light of Nature*. There is, to be sure, a certain light of nature remaining in man after the fall, by virtue of which he retains some notions about God, natural things, and the difference between what is moral and immoral, and demonstrates a certain eagerness for virtue and for good outward behavior. But this light of nature is far from enabling man to come to a saving knowledge of God and conversion to him – so far, in fact, that man does not use it rightly even in matters of nature and society. Instead, in various ways he completely distorts this light, whatever its precise character, and suppresses it in unrighteousness. In doing so he renders himself without excuse before God.

Article 5: *The Inadequacy of the Law*. In this respect, what is true of the light of nature is true also of the Ten Commandments given by God through Moses specifically to the Jews. For man cannot obtain saving grace through the Decalogue, because, although it does expose the magnitude of his sin and increasingly convict him of his guilt, yet it does not offer a remedy or enable him to escape from his misery, and, indeed, weakened as it is by the flesh, leaves the offender under the curse.

Article 6: *The Saving Power of the Gospel.* What, therefore, neither the light of nature nor the law can do, God accomplishes by the power of the Holy Spirit, through the Word or the ministry of reconciliation. This is the gospel about the Messiah, through which it has pleased God to save believers, in both the Old and the New Testament.

Article 7: *God's Freedom in Revealing the Gospel.* In the Old Testament, God revealed this secret of his will to a small number; in the New Testament (now without any distinction between peoples) he discloses it to a large number. The reason for this difference must not be ascribed to the greater worth of one nation over another, or to a better use of the light of nature, but to the free good pleasure and undeserved love of God. Therefore, those who receive so much grace, beyond and in spite of all they deserve, ought to acknowledge it with humble and thankful hearts; on the other hand, with the apostle they ought to adore (but certainly not inquisitively search into) the severity and justice of God's judgments on the others, who do not receive this grace.

Article 8: *The Serious Call of the Gospel.* Nevertheless, all who are called through the gospel are called seriously. For seriously and most genuinely God makes known in his Word what is pleasing to him: that those who are called should come to him. Seriously he also promises rest for their souls and eternal life to all who come to him and believe.

Article 9: *Human Responsibility for Rejecting the Gospel.* The fact that many who are called through the ministry of the gospel do not come and are not brought to conversion must not be blamed on the gospel, nor on Christ, who is offered through the gospel, nor on God, who calls them through the gospel and even bestows various gifts on them, but on the people themselves who are called. Some in self-assurance do not even entertain the Word of life; others do entertain it but do not take it to heart, and for that reason, after the fleeting joy of a temporary faith, they relapse; others choke the seed of the Word with the thorns of life's cares and with the pleasures of the world and bring forth no fruits. This our Savior teaches in the parable of the sower (Matt. 13).

Article 10: *Conversion as the Work of God.* The fact that others who are called through the ministry of the gospel do come and are brought to conversion must not be credited to man, as though one distinguishes himself by free choice from others who are furnished with equal or sufficient grace for faith and conversion (as the proud heresy of Pelagius maintains). No, it must be credited to God: just as from eternity he chose his own in Christ, so within time he effectively calls them, grants them faith and repentance, and, having rescued them from the dominion of darkness, brings them into the kingdom of his Son, in order that they may declare the wonderful deeds of him who called them out of darkness into this marvelous light, and may boast not in themselves, but in the Lord, as apostolic words frequently testify in Scripture.

Article 11: *The Holy Spirit's Work in Conversion.* Moreover, when God carries out this good pleasure in his chosen ones, or works true conversion in them, he not only sees to it that the gospel is proclaimed to them outwardly, and enlightens their minds powerfully by the Holy Spirit so that they may rightly understand and discern the things of the Spirit of God, but, by the effective operation of the same regenerating Spirit, he also penetrates into the inmost being of man, opens the closed heart, softens the hard heart, and circumcises the heart that is uncircumcised. He infuses new qualities into the will, making the dead will alive, the evil one good, the unwilling one willing, and the stubborn one compliant; he activates and strengthens the will so that, like a good tree, it may be enabled to produce the fruits of good deeds.

Article 12: *Regeneration a Supernatural Work*. And this is the regeneration, the new creation, the raising from the dead, and the making alive so clearly proclaimed in the Scriptures, which God works in us without our help. But this certainly does not happen only by outward teaching, by moral persuasion, or by such a way of working that, after God has done his work, it remains in man's power whether or not to be reborn or converted. Rather, it is an entirely supernatural work, one that is at the same time most powerful and most pleasing, a marvelous, hidden, and inexpressible work, which is not lesser than or inferior in power to that of creation or of raising the dead, as Scripture (inspired by the author of this work) teaches. As a result, all those in whose hearts God works in this marvelous way are certainly, unfailingly, and effectively reborn and do actually believe. And then the will, now renewed, is not only activated and motivated by God but in being activated by God is also itself active. For this reason, man himself, by that grace which he has received, is also rightly said to believe and to repent.

Article 13: *The Incomprehensible Way of Regeneration*. In this life believers cannot fully understand the way this work occurs; meanwhile, they rest content with knowing and experiencing that by this grace of God they do believe with the heart and love their Savior.

Article 14: *The Way God Gives Faith*. In this way, therefore, faith is a gift of God, not in the sense that it is offered by God for man to choose, but that it is in actual fact bestowed on man, breathed and infused into him. Nor is it a gift in the sense that God bestows only the potential to believe, but then awaits assent – the act of believing – from man's choice; rather, it is a gift in the sense that he who works both willing and acting and, indeed, works all things in all people produces in man both the will to believe and the belief itself.

Article 15: *Responses to God's Grace*. God does not owe this grace to anyone. For what could God owe to one who has nothing to give that can be paid back? Indeed, what could God owe to one who has nothing of his own to give but sin and falsehood? Therefore the person who receives this grace owes and gives eternal thanks to God alone; the person who does not receive it either does not care at all about these spiritual things and is satisfied with himself in his condition, or else in self-assurance foolishly boasts about having something which he lacks. Furthermore, following the example of the apostles, we are to think and to speak in the most favorable way about those who outwardly profess their faith and better their lives, for the inner chambers of the heart are unknown to us. But for others who have not yet been called, we are to pray to the God who calls things that do not exist as though they did. In no way, however, are we to pride ourselves as better than they, as though we had distinguished ourselves from them.

Article 16: *Regeneration's Effect*. However, just as by the fall man did not cease to be man, endowed with intellect and will, and just as sin, which has spread through the whole human race, did not abolish the nature of the human race but distorted and spiritually killed it, so also this divine grace of regeneration does not act in people as if they were blocks and stones; nor does it abolish the will and its properties or coerce a reluctant will by force, but spiritually revives, heals, reforms, and – in a manner at once pleasing and powerful – bends it back. As a result, a ready and sincere obedience of the Spirit now begins to prevail where before the rebellion and resistance of the flesh were completely dominant. It is in this that the true and spiritual restoration and freedom of our will consists. Thus, if the marvelous Maker of every good thing were not dealing with us, man would have no hope of getting up from his fall by his free choice, by which he plunged himself into ruin when still standing upright.

Article 17: *God's Use of Means in Regeneration*. Just as the almighty work of God by which he brings forth and sustains our natural life does not rule out but requires the use of means, by which God, according to his infinite wisdom and goodness, has wished to exercise his power, so also the aforementioned supernatural work of God by which he regenerates us in no way rules out or cancels the use of the gospel, which God in his great wisdom has appointed to be the seed of regeneration and the food of the soul. For this reason, the apostles and the teachers who followed them taught the people in a godly manner about this grace of God, to give him the glory and to humble all pride, and yet did not neglect meanwhile to keep the people, by means of the holy admonitions of the gospel, under the administration of the Word, the sacraments, and discipline. So even today it is out of the question that the teachers or those taught in the church should presume to test God by separating what he in his good pleasure has wished to be closely joined together. For grace is bestowed through admonitions, and the more readily we perform our duty, the more lustrous the benefit of God working in us usually is and the better his work advances. To him alone, both for the means and for their saving fruit and effectiveness, all glory is owed forever. Amen.

Rejection of Errors

Having set forth the orthodox teaching, the Synod rejects the errors of those –

First. Who teach that, properly speaking, it cannot be said that original sin in itself is enough to condemn the whole human race or to warrant temporal and eternal punishments.

For they contradict the apostle when he says: "Sin entered the world through one man, and death through sin, and in this way death passed on to all men because all sinned" (Rom. 5:12); also: "The guilt followed one sin and brought condemnation" (Rom. 5:16); likewise: "The wages of sin is death" (Rom. 6:23).

Second. Who teach that the spiritual gifts or the good dispositions and virtues such as goodness, holiness, and righteousness could not have resided in man's will when he was first created, and therefore could not have been separated from the will at the fall.

For this conflicts with the apostle's description of the image of God in Ephesians 4:24, where he portrays the image in terms of righteousness and holiness, which definitely reside in the will.

Third. Who teach that in spiritual death the spiritual gifts have not been separated from man's will, since the will in itself has never been corrupted but only hindered by the darkness of the mind and the unruliness of the emotions, and since the will is able to exercise its innate free capacity once these hindrances are removed, which is to say, it is able of itself to will or choose whatever good is set before it – or else not to will or choose it.

This is a novel idea and an error and has the effect of elevating the power of free choice, contrary to the words of Jeremiah the prophet: "The heart itself is deceitful above all things and wicked" (Jer. 17:9); and of the words of the apostle: "All of us also lived among them (the sons of dis-obedience) at one time in the passions of our flesh, following the will of our flesh and thoughts" (Eph. 2:3).

Fourth. Who teach that unregenerate man is not strictly or totally dead in his sins or deprived of all capacity for spiritual good but is able to hunger and thirst for righteous-ness or life and to offer the sacrifice of a broken and contrite spirit which is pleasing to God.

For these views are opposed to the plain testimonies of Scripture: "You were dead in your transgressions and sins" (Eph. 2:1, 5); "The imagination of the thoughts of man's heart is only evil all the time" (Gen. 6:5; 8:21). Besides, to hunger and thirst for deliverance from misery and for life, and to offer God the sacrifice of a broken spirit is characteristic only of the regenerate and of those called blessed (Ps. 51:17; Matt. 5:6).

Fifth. Who teach that corrupt and natural man can make such good use of common grace (by which they mean the light of nature) or of the gifts remaining after the fall that he is able thereby gradually to obtain a greater grace – evangelical or saving grace – as well as salvation itself; and that in this way God, for his part, shows himself ready to reveal Christ to all people, since he provides to all, to a sufficient extent and in an effective manner, the means necessary for the revealing of Christ, for faith, and for repentance.

For Scripture, not to mention the experience of all ages, testifies that this is false: "He makes known his words to Jacob, his statutes and his laws to Israel; he has done this for no other nation, and they do not know his laws" (Ps. 147:19-20); "In the past God let all nations go their own way" (Acts 14:16); "They [Paul and his companions] were kept by the Holy Spirit from speaking God's word in Asia; and "When they had come to Mysia, they tried to go to Bithynia, but the Spirit would not allow them to" (Acts 16:6-7).

Sixth. Who teach that in the true conversion of man new qualities, dispositions, or gifts cannot be infused or poured into his will by God, and indeed that the faith by which we first come to conversion and from which we receive the name "believers" is not a quality or gift infused by God, but only an act of man, and that it cannot be called a gift except in respect to the power of attaining faith.

For these views contradict the Holy Scriptures, which testify that God does infuse or pour into our hearts the new qualities of faith, obedience, and the experiencing of his love: "I will put my law in their minds, and write it on their hearts" (Jer. 31:33); "I will pour water on the thirsty land, and streams on the dry ground; I will pour out my Spirit on your offspring" (Isa. 44:3); "The love of God has been poured out in our hearts by the Holy Spirit, who has been given to us" (Rom. 5:5). They also conflict with the continuous practice of the Church, which prays with the prophet: "Convert me, LORD, and I shall be converted" (Jer. 31:18).

Seventh. Who teach that the grace by which we are converted to God is nothing but a gentle persuasion, or (as others explain it) that the way of God's acting in man's conversion that is most noble and suited to human nature is that which happens by persuasion, and that nothing prevents this grace of moral suasion even by itself from making natural men spiritual; indeed, that God does not produce the assent of the will except in this manner of moral suasion, and that the effectiveness of God's work by which it surpasses the work of Satan consists in the fact that God promises eternal benefits while Satan promises temporal ones.

For this teaching is entirely Pelagian and contrary to the whole of Scripture, which recognizes besides this persuasion also another, far more effective and divine way in which the Holy Spirit acts in man's conversion. As Ezekiel 36:26 puts it: "I will give you a new heart and put a new spirit in you; and I will remove your heart of stone and give you a heart of flesh. . . ."

Eighth. Who teach that God in regenerating man does not bring to bear that power of his omnipotence whereby he may powerfully and unfailingly bend man's will to faith and conversion, but that even when God has accomplished all the works of grace which he uses for man's conversion, man nevertheless can, and in actual fact often does, so resist God and the Spirit in their intent and will to regenerate him, that man completely thwarts his own rebirth; and, indeed, that it remains in his own power whether or not to be reborn.

For this does away with all effective functioning of God's grace in our conversion and subjects the activity of Almighty God to the will of man; it is contrary to the apostles, who teach that we believe by virtue of the effective working of God's mighty strength (Eph. 1:19), and that God fulfills the undeserved good will of his kindness and the work of faith in us with power (2 Thess. 1:11), and likewise that his divine power has given us everything we need for life and godliness (2 Pet. 1:3).

Ninth. Who teach that grace and free choice are concurrent partial causes which cooperate to initiate conversion, and that grace does not precede – in the order of causality – the effective influence of the will; that is to say, that God does not effectively help man's will to come to conversion before man's will itself motivates and determines itself.

For the early church already condemned this doctrine long ago in the Pelagians, on the basis of the words of the apostle: "It does not depend on man's willing or running but on God's mercy" (Rom. 9:16); also: "Who makes you different from anyone else?" and "What do you have that you did not receive?" (1 Cor. 4:7); likewise: "It is God who works in you to will and act according to his good pleasure" (Phil. 2:13).

Fifth Head of Doctrine:
The Perseverance of the Saints

Article 1: *The Regenerate Not Entirely Free from Sin.* Those people whom God according to his purpose calls into fellowship with his Son Jesus Christ our Lord and regenerates by the Holy Spirit, he also sets free from the reign and slavery of sin, though in this life not entirely from the flesh and from the body of sin.

Article 2: *The Believer's Reaction to Sins of Weakness.* Hence daily sins of weakness arise, and blemishes cling to even the best works of God's people, giving them continual cause to humble themselves before God, to flee for refuge to Christ crucified, to put the flesh to death more and more by the Spirit of supplication and by holy exercises of godliness, and to strain toward the goal of perfection, until they are freed from this body of death and reign with the Lamb of God in heaven.

Article 3: *God's Preservation of the Converted.* Because of these remnants of sin dwelling in them and also because of the temptations of the world and Satan, those who have been converted could not remain standing in this grace if left to their own resources. But God is faithful, mercifully strengthening them in the grace once conferred on them and powerfully preserving them in it to the end.

Article 4: *The Danger of True Believers' Falling Into Serious Sins.* Although that power of God strengthening and preserving true believers in grace is more than a match for the flesh, yet those converted are not always so activated and motivated by God that in certain specific actions they cannot by their own fault depart from the leading of grace, be led astray by the desires of the flesh, and give in to them. For this reason they must constantly watch and pray that they may not be led into temptations. When they fail to do this, not only can they be carried away by the flesh, the world, and Satan into sins, even serious and outrageous ones, but also by God's just permission they sometimes are so carried away – witness the sad cases, described in Scripture, of David, Peter, and other saints falling into sins.

Article 5: *The Effects of Such Serious Sins*. By such monstrous sins, however, they greatly offend God, deserve the sentence of death, grieve the Holy Spirit, suspend the exercise of faith, severely wound the conscience, and sometimes lose the awareness of grace for a time – until, after they have returned to the way by genuine repentance, God's fatherly face again shines upon them.

Article 6: *God's Saving Intervention*. For God, who is rich in mercy, according to his unchangeable purpose of election does not take his Holy Spirit from his own completely, even when they fall grievously. Neither does he let them fall down so far that they forfeit the grace of adoption and the state of justification, or commit the sin which leads to death (the sin against the Holy Spirit), and plunge themselves, entirely forsaken by him, into eternal ruin.

Article 7: *Renewal to Repentance*. For, in the first place, God preserves in those saints when they fall his imperishable seed from which they have been born again, lest it perish or be dislodged. Secondly, by his Word and Spirit he certainly and effectively renews them to repentance so that they have a heartfelt and godly sorrow for the sins they have committed; seek and obtain, through faith and with a contrite heart, forgiveness in the blood of the Mediator; experience again the grace of a reconciled God; through faith adore his mercies; and from then on more eagerly work out their own salvation with fear and trembling.

Article 8: *The Certainty of This Preservation.* So it is not by their own merits or strength but by God's undeserved mercy that they neither forfeit faith and grace totally nor remain in their downfalls to the end and are lost. With respect to themselves this not only easily could happen, but also undoubtedly would happen; but with respect to God it cannot possibly happen, since his plan cannot be changed, his promise cannot fail, the calling according to his purpose cannot be revoked, the merit of Christ as well as his interceding and preserving cannot be nullified, and the sealing of the Holy Spirit can neither be invalidated nor wiped out.

Article 9: *The Assurance of This Preservation.* Concerning this preservation of those chosen to salvation and concerning the perseverance of true believers in faith, believers themselves can and do become assured in accordance with the measure of their faith, by which they firmly believe that they are and always will remain true and living members of the church, and that they have the forgiveness of sins and eternal life.

Article 10: *The Ground of This Assurance.* Accordingly, this assurance does not derive from some private revelation beyond or outside the Word, but from faith in the promises of God which he has very plentifully revealed in his Word for our comfort, from the testimony of the Holy Spirit testifying with our spirit that we are God's children and heirs (Rom. 8:16-17), and finally from a serious and holy pursuit of a clear conscience and of good works. And if God's chosen ones in this world did not have this well-founded comfort that the victory will be theirs and this reliable guarantee of eternal glory, they would be of all people most miserable.

Article 11: *Doubts Concerning This Assurance*. Meanwhile, Scripture testifies that believers have to contend in this life with various doubts of the flesh and that under severe temptation they do not always experience this full assurance of faith and certainty of perseverance. But God, the Father of all comfort, does not let them be tempted beyond what they can bear, but with the temptation he also provides a way out (1 Cor. 10:13), and by the Holy Spirit revives in them the assurance of their perseverance.

Article 12: *This Assurance as an Incentive to Godliness*. This assurance of perseverance, however, so far from making true believers proud and carnally self-assured, is rather the true root of humility, of childlike respect, of genuine godliness, of endurance in every conflict, of fervent prayers, of steadfastness in crossbearing and in confessing the truth, and of well-founded joy in God. Reflecting on this benefit provides an incentive to a serious and continual practice of thanksgiving and good works, as is evident from the testimonies of Scripture and the examples of the saints.

Article 13: *Assurance No Inducement to Carelessness*. Neither does the renewed confidence of perseverance produce immorality or lack of concern for godliness in those put back on their feet after a fall, but it produces a much greater concern to observe carefully the ways of the Lord which he prepared in advance. They observe these ways in order that by walking in them they may maintain the assurance of their perseverance, lest, by their abuse of his fatherly goodness, the face of the gracious God (for the godly, looking upon his face is sweeter than life, but its withdrawal is more bitter than death) turn away from them again, with the result that they fall into greater anguish of spirit.

Article 14: *God's Use of Means in Perseverance*. And, just as it has pleased God to begin this work of grace in us by the proclamation of the gospel, so he preserves, continues, and completes his work by the hearing and reading of the gospel, by meditation on it, by its exhortations, threats, and promises, and also by the use of the sacraments.

Article 15: *Contrasting Reactions to the Teaching of Perseverance*. This teaching about the perseverance of true believers and saints, and about their assurance of it – a teaching which God has very richly revealed in his Word for the glory of his name and for the comfort of the godly and which he impresses on the hearts of believers – is something which the flesh does not understand, Satan hates, the world ridicules, the ignorant and the hypocrites abuse, and the spirits of error attack. The bride of Christ, on the other hand, has always loved this teaching very tenderly and defended it steadfastly as a priceless treasure; and God, against whom no plan can avail and no strength can prevail, will ensure that she will continue to do this. To this God alone, Father, Son, and Holy Spirit, be honor and glory forever. Amen.

Rejection of Errors

Having set forth the orthodox teaching, the Synod rejects the errors of those –

First. Who teach that the perseverance of true believers is not an effect of election or a gift of God produced by Christ's death, but a condition of the new covenant which man, before what they call his "peremptory" election and justification, must fulfill by his free will.

For Holy Scripture testifies that perseverance follows from election and is granted to the chosen by virtue of Christ's death, resurrection, and intercession: "The chosen obtained it; the others were hardened" (Rom. 11:7); likewise, "He who did not spare his own son, but gave him up for us all – how will he not, along with him, grant us all things? Who will bring any charge against those whom God has chosen? It is God who justifies. Who is he that condemns? It is Christ Jesus who died – more than that, who was raised – who also sits at the right hand of God, and is also interceding for us. Who shall separate us from the love of Christ?" (Rom. 8:32-35).

Second. Who teach that God does provide the believer with sufficient strength to persevere and is ready to preserve this strength in him if he performs his duty, but that even with all those things in place which are necessary to persevere in faith and which God is pleased to use to preserve faith, it still always depends on the choice of man's will whether or not he perseveres.

For this view is obviously Pelagian; and though it intends to make men free it makes them sacrilegious. It is against the enduring consensus of evangelical teaching which takes from man all cause for boasting and ascribes the praise for this benefit only to God's grace. It is also against the testimony of the apostle: "It is God who keeps us strong to the end, so that we will be blameless on the day of our Lord Jesus Christ" (1 Cor. 1:8).

Third. Who teach that those who truly believe and have been born again not only can forfeit justifying faith as well as grace and salvation totally and to the end, but also in actual fact do often forfeit them and are lost forever.

For this opinion nullifies the very grace of justification and regeneration as well as the continual preservation by Christ, contrary to the plain words of the apostle Paul: "If Christ died for us while we were still sinners, we will therefore much more be saved from God's wrath through him, since we have now been justified by his blood" (Rom. 5:8-9); and contrary to the apostle John: "No one who is born of God is intent on sin, because God's seed remains in him, nor can he sin, because he has been born of God" (1 John 3:9); also contrary to the words of Jesus Christ: "I give eternal life to my sheep, and they shall never perish; no one can snatch them out of my hand. My Father, who has given them to me, is greater than all; no one can snatch them out of my Father's hand" (John 10:28-29).

Fourth. Who teach that those who truly believe and have been born again can commit the sin that leads to death (the sin against the Holy Spirit).

For the same apostle John, after making mention of those who commit the sin that leads to death and forbidding prayer for them (1 John 5:16-17), immediately adds: "We know that anyone born of God does not commit sin (that is, that kind of sin), but the one who was born of God keeps himself safe, and the evil one does not touch him" (v. 18).

Fifth. Who teach that apart from a special revelation no one can have the assurance of future perseverance in this life.

For by this teaching the well-founded consolation of true believers in this life is taken away and the doubting of the Romanists is reintroduced into the church. Holy Scripture, however, in many places derives the assurance not from a special and extraordinary revelation but from the marks peculiar to God's children and from God's completely reliable promises. So especially the apostle Paul: "Nothing in all creation can separate us from the love of God that is in Christ Jesus our Lord" (Rom. 8:39); and John: "They who obey his commands remain in him and he in them. And this is how we know that he remains in us: by the Spirit he gave us" (1 John 3:24).

Sixth. Who teach that the teaching of the assurance of perseverance and of salvation is by its very nature and character an opiate of the flesh and is harmful to godliness, good morals, prayer, and other holy exercises, but that, on the contrary, to have doubt about this is praiseworthy.

For these people show that they do not know the effective operation of God's grace and the work of the indwelling Holy Spirit, and they contradict the apostle John, who asserts the opposite in plain words: "Dear friends, now we are children of God, but what we will be has not yet been made known. But we know that when he is made known, we shall be like him, for we shall see him as he is. Everyone who has this hope in him purifies himself, just as he is pure" (1 John 3:2-3). Moreover, they are refuted by the examples of the saints in both the Old and the New Testament, who though assured of their perseverance and salvation yet were constant in prayer and other exercises of godliness.

Seventh. Who teach that the faith of those who believe only temporarily does not differ from justifying and saving faith except in duration alone.

For Christ himself in Matthew 13:20ff. and Luke 8:13ff. clearly defines these further differences between temporary and true believers: he says that the former receive the seed on rocky ground, and the latter receive it in good ground, or a good heart; the former have no root, and the latter are firmly rooted; the former have no fruit, and the latter produce fruit in varying measure, with steadfastness, or perseverance.

Eighth. Who teach that it is not absurd that a person, after losing his former regeneration, should once again, indeed quite often, be reborn.

For by this teaching they deny the imperishable nature of God's seed by which we are born again, contrary to the testimony of the apostle Peter: "Born again, not of perishable seed, but of imperishable" (1 Pet. 1:23).

Ninth. Who teach that Christ nowhere prayed for an unfailing perseverance of believers in faith.

For they contradict Christ himself when he says: "I have prayed for you, Peter, that your faith may not fail" (Luke 22:32); and John the gospel writer when he testifies in John 17 that it was not only for the apostles, but also for all those who were to believe by their message that Christ prayed: "Holy Father, preserve them in your name" (v. 11); and "My prayer is not that you take them out of the world, but that you preserve them from the evil one" (v. 15).

Conclusion:
Rejection of False Accusations

And so this is the clear, simple, and straightforward explanation of the orthodox teaching on the five articles in dispute in the Netherlands, as well as the rejection of the errors by which the Dutch churches have for some time been disturbed. This explanation and rejection the Synod declares to be derived from God's Word and in agreement with the confessions of the Reformed churches. Hence it clearly appears that those of whom one could hardly expect it have shown no truth, equity, and charity at all in wishing to make the public believe:

– that the teaching of the Reformed churches on predestination and on the points associated with it by its very nature and tendency draws the minds of people away from all godliness and religion, is an opiate of the flesh and the devil, and is a stronghold of Satan where he lies in wait for all people, wounds most of them, and fatally pierces many of them with the arrows of both despair and self-assurance;

– that this teaching makes God the author of sin, unjust, a tyrant, and a hypocrite; and is nothing but a refurbished Stoicism, Manicheism, Libertinism, and Mohammedanism;

– that this teaching makes people carnally self-assured, since it persuades them that nothing endangers the salvation of the chosen, no matter how they live, so that they may commit the most outrageous crimes with self-assurance; and that on the other hand nothing is of use to the reprobate for salvation even if they have truly performed all the works of the saints;

– that this teaching means that God predestined and created, by the bare and unqualified choice of his will, without the least regard or consideration of any sin, the greatest part of the world to eternal condemnation; that in the same manner in which election is the source and cause of faith and good works, reprobation is the cause of unbelief and ungodliness; that many infant children of believers are snatched in their innocence from their mothers' breasts and cruelly cast into hell so that neither the blood of Christ nor their baptism nor the prayers of the church at their baptism can be of any use to them; and very many other slanderous accusations of this kind which the Reformed churches not only disavow but even denounce with their whole heart.

Therefore this Synod of Dordt in the name of the Lord pleads with all who devoutly call on the name of our Savior Jesus Christ to form their judgment about the faith of the Reformed churches, not on the basis of false accusations gathered from here or there, or even on the basis of the personal statements of a number of ancient and modern authorities – statements which are also often either quoted out of context or misquoted and twisted to convey a different meaning – but on the basis of the churches' own official confessions and of the present explanation of the orthodox teaching which has been endorsed by the unanimous consent of the members of the whole Synod, one and all.

Moreover, the Synod earnestly warns the false accusers themselves to consider how heavy a judgment of God awaits those who give false testimony against so many churches and their confessions, trouble the consciences of the weak, and seek to prejudice the minds of many against the fellowship of true believers.

Finally, this Synod urges all fellow ministers in the gospel of Christ to deal with this teaching in a godly and reverent manner, in the academic institutions as well as in the churches; to do so, both in their speaking and writing, with a view to the glory of God's name, holiness of life, and the comfort of anxious souls; to think and also speak with Scripture according to the analogy of faith; and, finally, to refrain from all those ways of speaking which go beyond the bounds set for us by the genuine sense of the Holy Scriptures and which could give impertinent sophists a just occasion to scoff at the teaching of the Reformed churches or even to bring false accusations against it.

May God's Son Jesus Christ, who sits at the right hand of God and gives gifts to men, sanctify us in the truth, lead to the truth those who err, silence the mouths of those who lay false accusations against sound teaching, and equip faithful ministers of his Word with a spirit of wisdom and discretion, that all they say may be to the glory of God and the building up of their hearers. Amen.

APPENDIX TWO

Was Arminius an Arminian?

It is perhaps unfortunate that the name of Jacob Arminius has traditionally been associated with the doctrines of the Remonstrants since his own views were not nearly as radical. In fact, having studied under Theodore Beza, Calvin's successor at Geneva, Arminius adhered to many of the essential elements of the Reformed faith. For example, it was his constant claim that he had "taught and wished to teach nothing that was in any wise repugnant to the [Belgic] Confession and [Heidelberg] Catechism,"[1] the two main creeds of the Reformed churches at that time. In Article XVI of the former, we find the following statement about "eternal election":

> We believe that all the posterity of Adam, being thus fallen into perdition and ruin by the sin of our first parents, God then did manifest himself such as he is; that is to say, merciful and just; merciful, since he delivers and preserves from this perdition all whom he, in his eternal and un-

---

1. James Arminius, *The Works of James Arminius* (Grand Rapids, Michigan: Baker Book House, 1986; James Nichols and William Nichols, translators), Volume I, page 106.

changeable council, of mere goodness hath elected in Christ
Jesus our Lord, without any respect to their works; just,
in leaving others in the fall and perdition wherein they
have involved themselves.

Arminius was very clear in explaining his interpretation
of this doctrine:

> ... [I]n his lapsed and sinful state, man is not capable,
> in and by himself, either to think, to will, or to do that
> which is really good; but it is necessary for him to be
> regenerated and renewed in his intellect, affections or will,
> and in all his powers, by God in Christ through the Holy
> Spirit, that he may be qualified rightly to understand,
> esteem, consider, will, and perform whatever is truly good.[2]

It is apparent, therefore, that Arminius did not have much
of a problem with accepting at least the first two points of
the Calvinistic system. It is also clear that he did not deny
the doctrine of the final perseverance of the saints, and, in
fact, held a view that was at least similar, if not identical,
to that of the Reformers of his day: "At no period have I
asserted that believers do finally decline or fall away from
faith or salvation."[3] Though he felt that he was not bound
by "the private interpretations of the Reformed,"[4] and though
he denounced the doctrine of "reprobation," Arminius nevertheless maintained a great respect for those men under whose
teachings he was schooled, particularly John Calvin himself:

---

2. Arminius, *ibid.*, page 659.

3. Arminius, *ibid.*, page 741.

4. Arminius, *ibid.*, page 103.

. . . [A]fter the Holy Scriptures, I exhort them [his students] to read the commentaries of Calvin, on whom I bestow higher praise than Helmichius ever did, as he confessed to me himself. For I tell them, that his commentaries ought to be held in greater estimation, than all that is delivered to us in the writings of the ancient Church Fathers: so that, in a certain eminent Spirit of Prophecy, I give the preeminence to him beyond most others, indeed beyond them all.[5]

Arminius was adamant in classifying himself amongst the Reformers in their denunciation of the Roman Catholic Church. His public statements regarding the Pope were equal to Calvin's in their castigation of the papacy: "I openly declare, that I do not own the Roman Pontiff to be a member of Christ's body; but I account him an enemy, a traitor, a sacrilegious and blasphemous man, a tyrant, and a violent usurper of most unjust domination over the Church, the man of sin, the son of perdition, that most notorious outlaw."[6]

Thus, it may be safely concluded that, unlike Calvinism, the Arminian system cannot be discovered in the writings and stated views of its namesake. In fact, though the moniker has been used throughout this book, "Arminian" is actually a misnomer, for Jacob Arminius himself would not qualify as one:

. . . [T]he most eminent of those who became Arminians, or who ranked among the professed followers of Arminius, soon adopted views of *the corruption of man, of justification, of the righteousness of Christ, of the nature of faith,*

---

5. Arminius, *ibid.*, page 295.

6. Arminius, *ibid.*, pages 298-299.

of the province of good works, and of the necessity and operations of grace, that are quite contrary to those which he had entertained and published. Many of them, in the process of time, differed more or less from one another, on all of these points. Even the Confession of Faith, which was drawn out for the Arminians by Episcopious, and is to be found in the second volume of his *Works,* cannot be referred to as a standard. It was composed merely to counteract the reproach of their being a society without any common principles. Every one was left entirely at liberty to interpret its language in the manner that was most agreeable to his own sentiments. Accordingly, so various and inconsistent are their opinions, that could Arminius peruse the unnumbered volumes which have been written as expositions and illustrations of Arminian doctrine, he would be at a loss to discover his own simple system, amidst that heterogeneous mass of error with which it has been rudely mixed; and would be astonished to find, that the controversy which he had unfortunately, but conscientiously, introduced, had wandered far from the point to which he had confined it, and that with his name dogmas were associated, the unscriptural and dangerous nature of which he had pointed out and condemned (emphasis in original).[7]

---

7. *Edinburgh Encyclopedia,* quoted in *ibid.,* page 306.

APPENDIX THREE
The Idolatry of Arminian Theology

The Essence of Idolatry

. . . [T]he idea that God knows and determines all things in advance and never has to adjust his planning is one that stands in obvious tension with the Bible and yet is deeply fixed in historic Christian thinking. It is due to the accommodation made in classic theism to the Hellenistic culture.[1]

So wrote Clark Pinnock regarding the doctrine of the immutability of God. Few Arminians would be comfortable with the lengths to which he has gone in developing his theology, and yet Pinnock is truer to Arminianism than most are willing to concede.

What of Pinnock's statement? Is the immutability of God simply a residue from Platonic philosophy, or does it, in fact, have a basis in Scripture? Is God's foreknowledge exhaustive or is He bound by the restrictions of time? At face value, these questions may not seem significant, but may it soon become apparent that the answer one gives to each of them

---

1. Pinnock, "From Augustine to Arminius," page 24.

will determine whether or not he has believed in the true God of the Bible or has instead created a god in his own image. In the words of A. W. Tozer:

> The essence of idolatry is the entertainment of thoughts about God that are unworthy of Him. It begins in the mind and may be present where no overt act of worship has taken place . . . . Wrong ideas about God are not only the fountain from which the polluted water of idolatry flow; they are themselves idolatrous. The idolater simply imagines things about God and acts as if they were true.[2]

Is God's Foreknowledge Merely Good Guesswork?

> . . . [I]t is highly important for us to have clear and scriptural views of the "foreknowledge" of God. Erroneous conceptions about it lead inevitably to thoughts most dishonouring to Him.[3]

In dealing with the subject of divine foreknowledge, we have only three options: (1) God foreknows all future events and therefore has foreordained them; (2) God foreknows all future events in such a way that He does not foreordain them, but merely witnesses them in advance; and (3) God does not foreknow all future events, and therefore neither foreordains them nor witnesses them in advance.

The first premise is that of Reformed theology. John Calvin explained that "single events are so regulated by God,

---

2. A. W. Tozer, *The Knowledge of the Holy* (New York: Harper Collins Publishers, 1961), pages 3-4.

3. A. W. Pink, *The Attributes of God* (Grand Rapids, Michigan: Baker Book House, 1975), page 27.

and all events so proceed from his determinate counsel, that nothing happens fortuitously."[4] Consequently, God "foresees the things which are to happen, simply because he decreed that they are so to happen . . . ."[5] The Westminster Confession similarly states: "God, from all eternity, did, by the most wise and holy counsel of his own will, freely, and unchangeably ordain whatsoever comes to pass . . . ."[6]

The classic Arminian objection to this doctrine is that it develops a fatalistic view of history that excludes human freedom. Thus, most Arminians will adopt the second option that God somehow foreknows the future without foreordaining it, not realizing that the implications thereof are virtually the same as those of the Calvinist position. The first premise defines the course of history as originating and existing within the sovereign control of God Himself. The past, present, and future are indeed set, but in this, the Calvinist finds his greatest peace, especially during times of tribulation.[7] Though

---

4. Calvin, *Institutes*, Book I, Chapter 16:4.

5. Calvin, *ibid.*, Book III, Chapter 23:6.

6. Westminster Confession, Chapter III:1.

7. John Calvin wrote the following:

> . . . [O]nce the light of Divine Providence has illumined the believer's soul, he is relieved and set free, not only from the extreme fear and anxiety which formerly oppressed him, but from all care. For as he justly shudders at the idea of chance, so he can confidently commit himself to God. This, I say, is his comfort, that his heavenly Father so embraces all things under his power – so governs them at will by his nod – so regulates them by his wisdom, that nothing takes place save according to his appointment; that received into his favour, and intrusted to the care of his angels, neither fire, nor water, nor sword, can do him harm, except in so far as God their master is pleased to permit (*Institutes*, Book I, Chapter 17:11).

it certainly is not intended as such, the second premise equally upholds the concept of a set history, though wresting it from the hands of divine control, and relegates God to merely a cosmic spectator of historical events rather than the Prime Mover thereof. After all, if God foreknows all things that will transpire, there must be a set of events for Him to foresee. The end result of such thinking is that time is an entity independent of God and is therefore self-existent.

Many Arminian writers themselves have acknowledged the difficulties inherent in this second option, causing them to ask the inevitable question: "If human beings are really free, and their actions are not determined by God, how can he know in advance everything they are going to do?"[8] Jacob Arminius himself was at a loss to adequately explain this: "The knowledge of God is eternal, immutable and infinite, and . . . extends to all things, both necessary and contingent. . . . But I do not understand the mode in which He knows future contingencies, and especially those which belong to the free-will of creatures. . . ."[9]

Hence, the only other option left to the Arminian critic of Calvinistic "determinism" is the third – God simply does not know what will happen in the future. This, unfortunately, is the position that is gaining wide acceptance among the new apologists for Arminianism. For example, Pinnock wrote:

> . . . I had to rethink the divine omniscience and reluctantly ask whether we ought to think of it as an exhaustive foreknowledge of everything that will ever happen, as even

---

8. Rice, "Divine Foreknowledge and Free Will Theism," page 123.

9. Arminius, *Writings*, Volume II, page 66.

most Arminians do. . . .

. . . I had to ask myself if it was biblically possible to
hold that God knows everything that can be known, but
that free choices would not be something that can be known
even by God because they are not yet settled in reality.
Decisions not yet made do not exist anywhere to be known
even by God. They are potential – yet to be realized but
not yet actual. God can predict a great deal of what we will
choose to do, but not all of it, because some of it remains
hidden in the mystery of human freedom.[10]

Pinnock also stated that ". . . God is not altogether sure
about the future and what he may have to do when it reveals
itself. . . ."[11] In other words, God can make a relatively good
guess about what may transpire, but He cannot be certain
of anything outside of events past and present. Thus, we
are left to view history as the result of impersonal causal
mechanisms that even God Himself cannot foresee or control.
In such a system, biblical prophecy becomes an absurdity.
According to Richard Rice, ". . . Biblical prophecy is not sheer
prognostication. . . . Its fundamental purpose is to reveal the
will of a personal being, declaring His intentions to accomplish certain things."[12]

This concept of deity is known as "process theology,"
due to the belief that, being limited to time and space, God
is incapable of knowing and controlling the future, and is
Himself, like man, involved in a process of learning and be-

---

10. Pinnock, "Augustine to Arminius," page 25.

11. Pinnock, *ibid.*, page 26.

12. Richard Rice, *God's Foreknowledge and Man's Free Will* (Bloomington,
Minnesota: Bethany House Publishers, 1985), page 77.

coming. According to Psalm 73:11, this is the wisdom of the wicked, not of the godly, and for that reason, process theology has been condemned as "horrible blasphemy"[13] and "a total capitulation to paganism."[14]

Does an Omniscient God Ever Change His Mind?

What then of the passages which speak of God changing His mind? Do not Genesis 6:5-6, Exodus 32:14, and other similar passages clearly indicate that man can act in such a way that was not anticipated by God, thus requiring Him to change His plans? It is true that these verses speak of God as being grieved by the actions of men, and the King James Version even uses the phrase "God repented." However, it is important to note that the Bible often portrays God's acts from the human perspective, and thus speaks figuratively of Him as if referring to a man. These references are known as *anthropomorphisms*, for they assign to God human characteristics to better relate His divine attributes to the reader. John Calvin explained: "Because our weakness cannot reach his height, any description which we receive of him must be lowered to our capacity in order to be intelligible. And the mode of lowering is to represent him not as he really is, but as we conceive of him."[15]

Lest this explanation be dismissed as fallible human reasoning, it may be helpful to return the passages in question to their proper context. Granted, Genesis 6:5-6 does

---

13. Pink, *Attributes of God*, page 14.

14. Ronald Nash, quoted in Robert A. Morey, *The Battle of the Gods* (Southbridge, Massachusetts: Crowne Publications, 1989), page 9.

15. Calvin, *Institutes*, Book I, Chapter 27:13.

indeed state that after "seeing" the wickedness of humanity, God was "grieved" that He had made man, but does it necessarily follow that God did not know that Adam and his descendants would fall into sin? In Revelation 13:8, we are told that Christ's atoning death for sinners was foreordained "from the creation of the world." It would be absurd to claim that God predetermined the solution to a problem that He did not foreknow would occur.

Likewise, in the account found in Exodus 32, Moses "reminded" God of His promise formerly made to Abraham and apparently persuaded Him not to destroy the rebellious Israelites in His anger. Did Moses' pleadings really change the mind of God, or was his faithfulness in his calling as leader of God's people merely being tested? Clearly, the latter is the case, for as Moses himself testified in Deuteronomy 10:10, "It was not His will to destroy [them]." These passages cannot be interpreted any other way, for the Bible does not contradict itself when it states, "God is not a man, that He should lie, nor a son of man, that He should repent. Has He said, and will He not do? Or has He spoken, and will He not make it good?" (Numbers 23:19).

Biblically speaking, if God is an eternal (timeless), self-existent, infinite and perfect Being, then His attributes, including His knowledge, must be likewise. An eternal knowledge does not have a point of origin, which means that God never begins to know something by learning, nor does His knowledge ever terminate in forgetfulness (Daniel 2:20-23). A self-existing knowledge indicates that God is not dependent upon others for what He knows (Isaiah 40:13-14). An infinite knowledge is one to which no limits can be assigned (Psalm 147:5), and a perfect knowledge is flawless and never has to be refined or "unlearned" (Job 37:16). Since there is nothing God does not know eternally, self-existently, infinitely, and perfectly, there can be no circumstance that God does not foreordain and control: "Because God knows all things perfectly, He knows no thing better than any other thing, but all things equally well. He never discovers anything, He is never surprised, never amazed. He never wonders about anything, nor (except when drawing men out for their own good) does He seek information or ask questions."[16]

The Biblical Definition of God's Decrees

> The decrees of God relate to all future things without exception: whatever is done in time was foreordained before time began. God's purpose was concerned with everything, whether great or small, whether good or evil. . . .[17]

Though the Arminian would define "God's decrees" as those things which He *wishes* to accomplish, but which are contingent upon the cooperation of His creatures, the Bible gives a very clear and contrary definition. Without exception, the right to decree is restricted in Scripture to those possessing sovereign authority. Hence, that which is willed or decreed by a potentate is that which is and must be carried out by his subjects. It was this royal prerogative that provided Daniel's enemies a vehicle by which to betray him, knowing well that King Darius' decree that all should worship him or perish would effectively doom the prophet to die in the lions' den. Even the king himself could not nul-

16. Tozer, *Knowledge of the Holy*, page 63.

17. Pink, *Attributes of God*, page 14.

lify his own decree to rescue Daniel (Daniel 6).

If the act of decreeing is to be thus understood with reference to earthly rulers, why then should we assume there is any difference in the decrees of God, who is "the blessed and only Potentate, the King of kings and Lord of lords" (1 Timothy 6:15)? According to Proverbs 21:1, "The king's heart is in the hand of the LORD, like the rivers of water; He turns it wherever He wishes." It certainly stands to reason that if the actions and wills of human kings, including their decrees, are so controlled by God as to always serve His purpose, then His own decrees cannot be inferior in quality and effectiveness: "I am the LORD, I do not change" (Malachi 3:6).

Actually, to speak of "God's decrees" is not entirely accurate. From the perspective of our own finite minds, which think in linear succession (one thought following another), a multiplicity of events require a sequence of thoughts. We are capable of considering only one circumstance at a time, and are thus bound to decision-making. God, on the other hand, who is not bound by the restraints of a temporal existence, looks upon time rather than dwells within it. He does not consider events in succession; He knows them all as a collective present:

> When we attribute prescience to God, we mean that all things always were, and ever continue, under his eye; that to his knowledge there is no past nor future, but all things are present, and indeed so present, that it is not merely the idea of them that is before him (as those objects are which we retain in our memory), but that he truly sees and contemplates them as actually under his immediate inspection. This prescience extends to the whole circuit of

the world, and to all creatures.[18]

Consequently, the Bible speaks of the "decree of the LORD" (Psalm 2:7), "His determined purpose" (Acts 4:28), "the counsel of His will" (Ephesians 1:11), etc., as one singular determination of all that has happened, is happening, and will happen in the realm of time. God's plan is utterly perfect in that it does not require revision of even its slightest detail and stands unperturbed by creaturely actions and wills: "Known to God from eternity are all His works" (Acts 15:18). Indeed, the God of the Calvinist is the all powerful, sovereign Lord of which the Scriptures attest, whose eternal decrees are as surely fulfilled as they are uttered from His mouth.

Is Calvinism a Form of Fatalism?

One of the most common accusations leveled against those who hold to the Calvinist understanding of divine sovereignty, or "placid predestinarianism," as it is derisively labeled, is that they "are guilty of an arbitrary, unlivable, and dangerous fatalism."[19] This mindset is best illustrated below by Randall Basinger:

> . . . [T]hose who attempt to act on the position that God is in sovereign control of events in their lives run into grave problems. At its best, this approach is unlivable. Why go to the doctor for anything? (If God wants us to be healthy, we will be healthy.) Why go to work? (If God wants us to have food and shelter, we will have food and shelter.) Why

---

18. Calvin, *Institutes*, Book III, Chapter 21:4.

19. Randall G. Basinger, "Exhaustive Divine Sovereignty: A Practical Critique," in Pinnock, *Grace of God/Will of Man*, page 196.

teach our children not to play with matches? (If God wants our children to be burned, they will be burned.). . . .

Moreover, at its worst, this theology is morally suspect. Why work for a nuclear freeze? (If God wants nuclear war, there will be nuclear war.) Why work against racial injustice? (If God wants people to have a job, they will have a job.) Why work on scientific research to explore the relationship between radiation exposure and birth defects? (If God want us to have a healthy baby, we will have a healthy baby.) If carried out consistently, this approach cuts the nerve of moral endeavor and leads the Christian into a passive life of moral resignation. What *is* will be what is right (emphasis in original).[20]

Such an argument is a false and uninformed caricature of what Reformed theology actually teaches. First of all, there is a vast difference between fatalism and the eternal decrees of God. In the former, men are merely puppets subject to the control of an impersonal force, while behind the divine decrees is an infinitely loving, just, and wise Person. Fatalism focuses solely upon the end; the means to the end are merely incidental. God, on the other hand, places equal emphasis upon both the means *and* the end as He "works all things according to the counsel of His will" (Ephesians 1:11). In other words, the means are as integral to His plan as is the end.[21]

---

20. Basinger, *ibid.*, page 195.

21. Calvin discussed this very issue at great length in his section on divine Providence found in the *Institutes*, Book I, Chapter 17. Here, he responded so directly to the objections raised here by Basinger that it is difficult to believe he has done any serious reading on the subject he presumes to criticize.

Charles Ryrie, though not a Calvinist, gave an excellent illustration of this:

> ... [D]oes God know the day you are going to die? The answer is yes. He does. Question: could you die a day sooner? The answer is no. Question: then why do you eat? Answer: to live. The means of eating is essential to the end of living to the preordained day of death. From this point on the illustration can easily and uselessly get into the realm of the hypothetical. Suppose I do not eat? Then I will die. Would that be the day God planned that I should die? These are questions that do not need to be asked or answered. Just eat.[22]

Does Calvinism Make God the Author of Evil?

> The logic of consistent Calvinism makes God the author of evil and casts serious doubt on his goodness. One is compelled to think of God's planning such horrors as Auschwitz, even though none but the most rigorous Calvinians can bring themselves to admit it.[23]

Again, this is a complete misrepresentation of true Calvinism. Did God foresee the "horrors of Auschwitz," or did they take Him by surprise? If the latter, then He most certainly suffers from the malady of temporality and can in no way be said to be eternal. If the former is the case, did He then lack the necessary power to stop the atrocities committed by the Nazis? Pinnock complained that absolute divine sovereignty renders God the "author of evil," and

---

22. Charles Ryrie, *Basic Theology* (Chicago, Illinois: Moody Press, 1986), page 318.

23. Pinnock, "Augustine to Arminius," page 21.

yet his position demands a god who is powerless to *stop* evil. Indeed, his own belief system is no more acceptable than the one he misconstrues Calvinism to be, for a truly sovereign God cannot be "dependent upon the uncontrollable actions of his own creatures."[24]

Calvinism does not, in fact, require that God be the author of evil, though His eternal decree has rendered it a necessary part of His plan. Since all of history is in one instant contemplated by the eternal God, He does not respond or react to chronological events, but rather orchestrates them (Isaiah 46:10). Hence, all that has happened, is happening, and will happen is contingent upon His unconditional and immutable decrees, and is subject to either His direct causation or His permissive will (Psalm 33:10-11; Ephesians 1:11). While the decree that sin should enter the creation is not the same as the decree to create – the former being permissive and the latter causative – one should not therefore assume that both were not the products of God's efficacious will. R.C. Sproul explained: "What we mean by the sovereign or efficacious will of God is that determination by which God sovereignly wills something to come to pass which therefore indeed does come to pass through the sheer efficacy, force, or power of that will."[25]

This, however, does not in any way absolve the sins of God's rational creatures, who, though acting according to His preordained plan, do so from the measure of freedom

---

24. A. A. Hodge, *Outlines of Theology* (New York: Robert Carter and Brothers, 1876), page 168.

25. R. C. Sproul, "Discerning the Will of God," in James M. Boice (editor), *Our Sovereign God* (Grand Rapids, Michigan: Baker Book House, 1977), page 105.

granted to them (Acts 2:22-23, 4:27-28). This freedom lies in the fact that God does not force men to act contrary to their own wills and desires, the dictating nature of which is sinful and depraved. For instance, Pharoah chose to repeatedly harden his heart against Moses and the Israelites because it was not in his nature to submit to the authority of God (Exodus 5:2, 8:15, 32). And yet, it would be foolish to claim that this was not in accordance with God's plan, for He had Himself hardened Pharoah's heart even before Moses entered his court to demand release of the Hebrew slaves (Exodus 4:21). To claim that God's actions were merely in response to those of Pharoah is to contradict such passages as Exodus 9:16, in which God declared, ". . . [I]ndeed for this purpose I have raised you up, that I may show My power in you, and that My name may be declared in all the earth."

Many other examples may be given of this divine co-operation with the fallen nature of man. The brothers of Joseph betrayed and sold him into slavery, and yet Joseph himself later acknowledged that it was not they who had sent him to Egypt, but God (Genesis 45:8). False prophets were rampant in Israel, and yet it was God Himself who had placed them there to test His people (Deuteronomy 13:3; Ezekiel 14:9). The Sabeans and Chaldeans plundered Job's home, killing his servants and stealing his livestock, and yet he gave praise to God, saying, "The LORD gave and the LORD has taken away" (Job 1:21). The Jewish leaders conspired together to have Christ put to death, yet they only accomplished what God's "purpose determined before to be done" (Acts 4:28). Finally, the reprobates of the world engage in all manner of sexual perversion and are "filled with all unrighteousness, sexual immorality, wickedness, covetousness, [and] maliciousness" (Romans 1:29), yet it is God who has decreed their actions by giving "them over to a debased [reprobate] mind" (Romans 1:28). Louis Berkhof explained:

> God's so ordering the universe that man will pursue a certain course of action, is . . . a quite different thing from His commanding him to do so. The decrees are not addressed to man, and are not the nature of statute law; neither do they impose compulsion or obligation on the wills of men. . . . The divine decrees are not addressed to men as a rule of action, and cannot be such a rule, since their contents become known only through, and therefore after, their realization.[26]

As Calvin pointed out, "man, though acted upon by God, at the same time also acts."[27] God simply directs the hearts of sinners in such a way that they act only according to their own pleasure. Pharoah would not have wished to voluntarily dismiss his slave labor force. Joseph's brothers were envious of his special relationship with their father Jacob. False prophets deliberately twist God's Word for selfish gain. The Sabeans and Chaldeans were barbarians and so had no regard for the property or lives of others. The Jews saw Christ as a threat to their religious authority. Unbelievers of their own accord refuse to submit themselves to the truth because of "the sinful desires of their hearts" (Romans 1:24). In this way, God cannot be said to be in any sense the author of evil, though evil cannot continue to exist apart from His sovereign directive, and is always employed as a means to the end of His own glory (Romans 8:28).

---

26. Berkhof, *Systematic Theology*, pages 103-107.

27. Calvin, *Institutes*, Book I, Chapter 18:2.

Conclusion

J.I. Packer once suggested "satanic malice and the natural darkness of the human mind" as the "contributory cause" of Arminian thinking.[28] Perhaps he was not far from the truth. The god of the consistent Arminian is a poor caricature of the God of the Bible, for he is one whose decrees are neither eternal nor certain, and in reality, are only the wistful dreams of perpetual impotence. It is small wonder that such a god stirs no great worship in the hearts of his devotees.

John Calvin was absolutely correct when he described the human imagination as "a perpetual forge of idols,"[29] for it will invariably attempt to manufacture a theology according to its own corruption if not governed and restrained by the authority of Scripture. In his persistent pride, fallen man simply refuses to accept the God he cannot fully understand, not realizing that he thereby creates another in his own image. In reality, such is no God at all, but merely man in divine attire, and the "religion" thereof merely atheism in pious disguise.

We close with the following warning: "Theology is not a game but a matter of eternal life or death. If you want a finite god, then you must choose Baal and serve him. But if you want to serve Jehovah, then you must accept Him as He has revealed Himself in the Bible."[30]

---

28. J.I. Packer, "Arminianisms," in W. Robert Godfrey and Jesse L. Boyd III (editors), *Through Christ's Word: A Festschrift For P. E. Hughes* (Phillipsburg, New Jersey: Presbyterian and Reformed Publishing Company, 1985), page 124.

29. Calvin, *Institutes*, Book I, Chapter 11:8.

30. Morey, *Battle of the Gods*, page 179.

APPENDIX FOUR
Imprisoned

I sat with hands and feet in chains
There in my musty cell;
If days were nights, or nights were days,
This I could not tell.
Then suddenly I heard them,
Steps approaching down the hall;
Not knowing why they came or who,
I pressed against the wall.

There He stood outside my cell,
His eyes were all aglow;
His count'nance shone with brilliant light,
From whence I did not know.
"Arise, my friend, the day has come
For you to be set free";
"Arise," again to me He said,
"And come and follow Me."

What foolishness is this? I thought,
I can't believe my ears!
"Shall I arise and walk," I asked,
"Having sat here all these years?

Can you not see the chains, dear Sir,
That keep me tightly bound?"
I waited for His answer, but
He just stood without a sound.

"Besides, my sentence," I went on,
"Has served to sap my will."
"I like it here," I said, as I,
Unmoving sat there still.
"Not so," He said, "for I've decreed
That you shall now be free.
You shall arise and leave this place,
And come and follow Me."

I perceived He had no key,
Yet He opened up the bars;
And as He reached His hands to me,
'Twas then I saw the scars.
"I loved you long ere you were born,
From everlasting, yea;
And laid My own life down for you
To set you free this day."

I felt within my soul a pow'r
That I could not resist;
I felt the chains fall to the ground,
My stubbornness desist.
My heart which once was stone within,
Was now a heart of flesh;
I scrambled up upon my feet,
My strength returned afresh.

I took His hand and wondered how
I ever thought it well,
To languish all alone there in
That dark and musty cell.
Down the hall and up the stairs,
I followed without doubt;
And from the darkness into light,
My Savior led me out.

BIBLIOGRAPHY

Arminius, James (Jacob), *The Works of James Arminius* (Grand Rapids, Michigan: Baker Book House, 1986).

Basinger, Randall and Basinger, David (editors), *Predestination and Free Will* (Downers Grove, Illinois: InterVarsity Press, 1986).

Berkhof, Louis, *History of Christian Doctrines* (Grand Rapids, Michigan: Wm. B. Eerdman's Publishing Company, 1937).

Berkhof, Louis, *Systematic Theology* (Grand Rapids, Michigan: Wm. B. Eerdman's Publishing Company, 1941).

Boettner, Loraine, *The Reformed Doctrine of Predestination* (Nutley, New Jersey: Presbyterian and Reformed Publishing Company, 1932).

Boettner, Loraine, *Studies in Theology* (Nutley, New Jersey: Presbyterian and Reformed Publishing Company, 1980).

Calvin, John, *Concerning the Eternal Predestination of God* (Cambridge, England: James Clarke and Company, Ltd., 1961).

Calvin, John, *Institutes of the Christian Religion* (Grand Rapids, Michigan: Wm. Eerdman's Publishing Company, 1989).

Calvin, John, *Commentaries on the Epistle to the Romans* (Grand Rapids, Michigan: Baker Book House, 1993).

Calvin, John, *Harmony of the Evangelists* (Grand Rapids, Michigan: Baker Book House, 1993).

Corner, Daniel, *The Believer's Security: Is It Unconditional?* (Washington, Pennsylvania: Evangelical Outreach, 1995).

Edwards, Jonathan, *Freedom of the Will* (New Haven, Connecticut: Yale University Press, 1957).

Erickson, Millard J., *Christian Theology* (Grand Rapids, Michigan: Baker Book House, 1985).

Ferguson, John, *Pelagius: An Historical and Theological Study* (New York, AMS Press, n.d.).

Gerstner, John, *A Predestinarian Primer* (Grand Rapids, Michigan: Baker Book House, 1960).

Gill, John, *The Cause of God and Truth* (Grand Rapids, Michigan: Sovereign Grace Publishers, 1971).

Gill, John, *A Complete Body of Doctrinal and Practical Divinity* (Paris, Arkansas: The Baptist Standard Bearer, 1987).

Godfrey, W. Robert and Boyd III, Jesse L. (editors), *Through Christ's Word: A Festschrift For P. E. Hughes* (Phillipsburg, New Jersey: Presbyterian and Reformed Publishing Company, 1985).

Graham, Billy, *How To Be Born Again* (Waco, Texas: Word Books, 1977).

Henry, Matthew, *Commentary on the Whole Bible* (Grand Rapids, Michigan: Zondervan Publishing House, 1961).

Hodge, Charles, *Systematic Theology* (Grand Rapids, Michigan: Wm. B. Eerdman's Publishing Company, 1993).

Hunt, Dave, *What Ever Happened to Heaven?* (Eugene, Oregon: Harvest House, 1990).

Hutson, Curtis, *Why I Disagree With All Five Points of Calvinism* (Murfreesboro, Tennessee: Sword of the Lord, 1980).

Lewis, C.S., *The Screwtape Letters* (New York: The Macmillan Company, Inc., 1961).

MacArthur, John, *The Gospel According to Jesus* (Grand Rapids, Michigan: Zondervan Publishing House, 1994).

Martin, A.W., *The Practical Implications of Calvinism* (Edinburgh, Scotland: The Banner of Truth Trust, 1979).

Matzat, Don, *Christ Esteem* (Eugene, Oregon: Harvest House Publishers, 1990).

Morris, Leon, *The Gospel According to John* (Grand Rapids, Michigan: Wm. B. Eerdman's Publishing Company, 1971).

Murray, Iain, *The Forgotten Spurgeon* (Edinburgh, Scotland: The Banner of Truth Trust, 1978).

Murray, Iain, *The Life of A. W. Pink* (Edinburgh, Scotland: The Banner of Truth Trust, 1981).

Owen, John, *The Death of Death in the Death of Christ* (Edinburgh, Scotland: The Banner of Truth Trust, 1985).

Owen, John, *The Works of John Owen, D.D.* (New York: Carter and Brothers, 1856).

Pearlman, Myer, *Knowing the Doctrines of the Bible* (Springfield, Missouri: Gospel Publishing House, 1937).

Pink, Arthur W., *An Exposition of Hebrews* (Grand Rapids, Michigan: Baker Book House, 1954).

Pink, Arthur W., *The Sovereignty of God* (Grand Rapids, Michigan: Baker Book House, 1984).

Pinnock, Clark H. (editor), *Grace Unlimited* (Minneapolis, Minnesota: Bethany House Publishers, 1975).

Pinnock, Clark H. (editor), *The Grace of God/The Will of Man* (Grand Rapids, Michigan: Zondervan Publishing House, 1989).

Ryrie, Charles C., *Basic Theology* (Wheaton, Illinois: Victor Books, 1986).

Schaff, Philip, *History of the Christian Church* (Grand Rapids, Michigan: Wm. B. Eerdman's Publishing Company, 1910).

Schaeffer, Frank, *Dancing Alone* (Brookline, Massachusetts: Holy Cross Orthodox Press, 1994).

Schuller, Robert H., *Self Esteem: The New Reformation* (Waco, Texas: Word Books, 1982).

Seaton, W. J., *The Five Points of Calvinism* (Edinburgh, Scotland: The Banner of Truth Trust, 1970).

Sell, Alan P., *The Great Debate* (Grand Rapids, Michigan: Baker Book House, 1982).

Sproul, R.C., *Chosen By God* (Wheaton, Illinois: Tyndale House Publishers, 1986).

Spurgeon, Charles Haddon, *C. H. Spurgeon's Autobiography* (Edinburgh, Scotland: The Banner of Truth Trust, 1962).

Stanley, Charles, *Eternal Security: Can You Be Sure?* (Nashville, Tennessee: Oliver-Nelson Books, 1990).

Strong, James, *A Concise Dictionary of the Words in the Hebrew Bible* (McLean, Virginia: MacDonald Publishing Company, n.d.).

Strong, James, *A Concise Dictionary of the Words in the Greek New Testament* (Maclean, Virginia: MacDonald Publishing Company, n.d.).

Strong, James, *A Greek Dictionary of the New Testament* (Grand Rapids, Michigan: Baker Book House, 1981).

Theissan, Henry C., *Introductory Lectures in Systematic Theology* (Grand Rapids, Michigan: Wm. B. Eerdman's Publishing Company, 1959).

Tozer, A. W., *The Pursuit of God* (Camp Hill, Pennsylvania: Christian Publications, Inc., 1982).

Vance, Laurence M., *The Other Side of Calvinism* (Pensacola, Florida: Vance Publications, 1991).

Vine, W. E., *Expository Dictionary of New Testament Words* (McLean, Virginia: MacDonald Publishing Company, n.d.).

Wesley, John, *The Works of the Reverend John Wesley* (New York: B. Waugh and T. Mason, 1833).

Wesley, John, *The Works of John Wesley* (Grand Rapids, Michigan: Baker Book House, 1979).

White, James, *Drawn By the Father* (Southbridge, Massachusetts: Crowne Publications, 1991).

SCRIPTURE INDEX

NAME INDEX

Abraham, William, 143
Arminius, Jacob, 11, 193ff, 200
Augustine, 11

Basinger, Randall, 206-207
Barth, Karl, 55
Berkhof, Louis, 81, 211
Beza, Theodore, 193
Boettner, Loraine, 12, 38, 64
Bunyan, John, 59

Calvin, John,
    Arminius' respect for, 194-195
    did not originate the five points, 10
    execution of Servetus, 9
    Institutes, 19
    mentioned, 45, 193
    on Adam's fall, 18
    on God's foreknowledge, 50-51, 205
    on God's foreordination, 198-199
    on God's self-revelation, 202
    on human nature, 15, 21, 27
    on human responsibility, 211
    on man's idolatry, 53, 212
    on justification, 53
    on limited atonement, 62-63
    on predestination, 38, 39
    on Providence, 199, 207
    on Romans 9, 52
    respect for Scripture, 9-10
Corner, Daniel, 120-121, 141-142
Craig, William L., 32

Davis, Stephen T., 28

Edwards, Jonathan, 23, 59
Episcopious, Simon, 11, 196

Geisler, Norman, 96-97, 115
Gerstner, John, 39
Gill, John, 38-39, 45, 51, 74, 78
Graham, Billy, 23, 103

Henn, Silas, 9
Henry, Matthew, 129, 135
Hodge, Charles, 25
Hodges, Zane, 140
Hunt, Dave, 43-44
Hutson, Curtis, 119-120

Lake, Donald M., 62-63, 73-74
Lewis, C. S., 103-104

MacArthur, John, 138-139
MacDonald, William, 58
Marshall, I. Howard, 65-66
Martin, A. W., 107
Miethe, Terry L., 8, 91
Morey, Robert, 212
Morris, Leon, 106
Murray, Ian, 147

Osteen, Joel, 16
Owen, John, 59, 63-64, 92-93, 102, 116-117, 149

Made in United States
Orlando, FL
14 January 2023